CLOWN

CLOWN

EMMETT KELLY

with F. Beverly Kelley

Decorations by Alicia Fiene

Prentice-Hall, Inc.

NEW YORK

12
Kelly

CONTENTS

29657

CLOWN

Friday, I tasted life. It was a vast morsel.
A Circus passed the house—still I feel the
red in my mind though the drums are out.

Emily Dickinson

COUNTRY BOY

Not long ago, between circus tours, I got on a
train that took me through Cabool, Missouri.

It is a little town, distinguished chiefly by its branch railroad, but there was a time when it was a farm boy's Bagdad,
Shangri-La and Broadway all rolled into one.

I was that boy. Our place was eighteen miles from
Cabool and about four miles from a smaller town, called
Houston, in Texas County, Missouri. It was in the Ozarks and
only about fifty-five miles from the Arkansas border.

This, however, was not my birthplace. I was born in
Sedan, Kansas, on December 9, 1898, in a house owned by
the Missouri-Pacific Railroad for which my father worked as
a section foreman.

Probably my mother sang to me as a baby, for she was
musically inclined, but my principal lullaby was the sounds
of the rolling cars, the clicking wheels and the lonely whistles
in the night. When I lie awake aboard the circus train as it
roars toward tomorrow's town, I hear the long wail of the
whistle and always it leads my mind back to the very early
days when I was the section boss' little boy.

9

My first name came from the middle name of the great Irish patriot, Robert Emmett. My mother wanted me named Leo, but my dad's wish prevailed and Leo became my second name. In school, the kids called me "The Irish Potater" or, finally, just "Tater" and it used to make me sore.

One of my early recollections, no doubt forecasting my wanderlust, is of being hauled out from under a string of freight cars after I had climbed our fence and run the short distance to the railroad siding. I did this several times, and somehow I escaped being run over when the cars were switched because a railroad man always found me and put me back in our yard where I belonged.

My father made exactly one dollar a day, and out of that he and my mother saved enough to buy their own home, a two-story frame not far from the section house. I was five at the time and had a baby sister, Sylvia, aged two. Our house had lilac trees in the yard and there was a cowshed where my mother kept a Jersey. So we had plenty of milk and butter and chickens of our own and a little garden. Mother worked hard from morning until night and sold most of the milk, butter and eggs.

I was five when I got the first spanking I remember. I had climbed a telephone pole and sat on the cross beam, which was no doubt my first rehearsal for the circus trapeze work I did much later. It was a lot higher than the tent where I did my first aerial work and of course it terrified my mother and the neighbors—and me, too, when they started to kick up a fuss. I did manage to climb about halfway down before they rescued me.

When I was in Portland, Oregon, not long ago with the Ringling show, a man came to "clown alley" and introduced himself to me as a former employee of my father's and also as one of the railroaders who recalls yanking me out from under the cars.

10

I remember well the band concerts every Saturday night in the public square in Sedan, but the last time I was there the bandstand was gone and nothing but a flagpole stood in its place. Sylvia and I ran away a few times to the concerts when our folks were too busy or too tired to take us, and while we generally were punished, I seem to remember it was worth it. I always loved the music of the band, and even now when the great circus bandmaster, Merle Evans, leads his boys into a break-neck galop I get bubbles in my blood.

Both my parents were born abroad. My father came from County Cork, Ireland; he never told us his exact age or anything much about Ireland except the beautiful hills back of his home. I remember one night in 1912 when he picked up his paper and read about the sinking of the *Titanic;* he said that he could have stood atop those hills on the southwestern tip of Ireland and looked out to the place where the ship had gone down.

He came to America alone when he was twenty-one and got a job as a hod carrier in New York City. While building a church, he and four men were lifting a heavy stone which had to be dressed, when the scaffold broke and dropped them seventy feet. Two were killed and one was badly hurt, but my father hit some scaffolding that broke his fall about halfway to the ground and probably saved his life. He had only some broken ribs and a broken collarbone from that fall.

As a young man, my father left New York and went out to Nebraska to become a railroader. In those days there was still some trouble with the Indians and the section gang kept rifles close at hand. In a southwestern Kansas town, he met my mother whose family ran a boardinghouse. Dad was somewhere past forty then and my mother was only eighteen. Her parents, Bohemians, disapproved of their romance, but they eloped and went to live in Sedan. Mother's family name was

11

Schimick and she had been born in Bohemia, but was brought to America as a baby.

My dad was medium height, stocky, square-shouldered and square-jawed with a sandy complexion and bushy eyebrows, curly hair and big ears like mine. He had a wide, rather flat nose and a full red mustache that he pulled a lot. He had blue eyes, the hands of a working man, but skin so tender that it would break at the slightest rubbing. I remember he had a fine sense of humor and loved jokes. His heavy, silver Waltham watch was almost a part of his skin, and I doubt if he was ever without it except when he went to bed. It is one of my most vivid memories of him and I still have it. Mother was short and plump with rather wide cheekbones and a pug nose like mine. She had a light complexion, her hair was brown and straight and her hands were small.

The railroad retired its employees at age sixty-five. One day I heard my dad say: "Hell, they'll never fire me; I'll quit first!" So before he reached retirement time, he had saved enough to make a substantial payment on a small farm in southern Missouri. We went to live on eighty acres in Texas County, where we stayed in a tent until the place we had bought from the Wheeler family was ready for us. I had never slept under canvas before; I didn't like it and neither did my sister. We cried ourselves to sleep, lonely for our old home. George Wheeler said he bet we were the only people in the world who were lonesome for Kansas.

Our new neighbor and his wife, Lulu, were mighty good to us. Wheeler fascinated us kids. He was a hunter, with a whole case of rifles. We ate our first deer meat with that family at one of their Sunday dinners to which we were often invited. They had the first phonograph I ever saw, with cylinder records and a goose-neck phone. We'd listen to records of Ada Jones, Uncle Josh and the marches of John Philip Sousa on Sunday afternoons. Wheeler had a magic lantern, too, and a telescope we could look into and see five miles down the valley.

The house we bought from the Wheelers had six rooms in two stories, with a gabled roof and a box stairway in the center. Sis and I each had our own room upstairs, and our parents slept on the first floor. Our barn was divided, one side for horses and the other for cattle and there was a sheep shed beyond the barn. Dad was sick at plowing time and I tried my best to help out, but I was so small that every time I'd get the blade into the ground, the horses would pull me right on over it. I was a total failure, and it looked as if we were in a real jam. However, that evening, Mother called me to the window and said, "I wonder what this can be." A team of horses and a farmer were dragging a plow up our drive. Another was close behind and another and another. Without so much as a word, those farmers quietly opened the barnyard gate and went into our big field and plowed it. I watched it all and it gave me a nice, warm feeling. Even now as I reflect on those untroubled days, I get a warm glow when I think of that old-fashioned neighborliness.

Our farm had huckleberries, blackberries, raspberries and grapes. There were peach trees, pear trees and two kinds of apples, as well as hickory nuts and walnuts. In our truck garden, we raised popcorn, watermelons and the long-necked muskmelons called "bananas"; we also had cabbages, onions, lettuce and radishes. In the spring, we would set aside one full day for "making the garden." This meant plowing and planning and sowing and it was an exciting time. Much later, I lived in a world of red wagons and billowing white tents that labored by a similar timetable. It had to do its whole job within the short space of a few hours—build itself new every day in a different town. Often it would remind me of the farm when we managed to put in the entire garden between dawn and dusk.

Our drinking water came from a spring a tenth of a mile from the house. The spring was built back in a hill and enclosed by rocks so that it was sheltered and there were steps down to it. My job was to keep the kitchen supplied with water. The spring never froze, even in the dead of winter, but in our kitchen we often had to break the ice with a dipper on cold mornings. On very cold nights, I slept in my underwear and the rest of the time in one of the flannel nightgowns my mother made for all the family. She would heat bricks in the oven on cold nights and put them at the foot of our beds. After a corn-bread breakfast (and nobody could cook it as my mother could), I'd go out and do the chores: take the horses and turn them loose, go down and fetch water from the spring for them to drink in the horsetrough, take the cows to the creek, often having to break the ice there so they could get to the water.

Winter and summer alike, we bathed on Saturday nights in a big tub in the kitchen. Mother filled it with hot water for each of us in turn; I hated it in wintertime because often the kitchen would get pretty cold late at night. But years after that, when I had learned to take a full bath out of a bucket of cold water on a chill Dixie night in a circus dressing tent, the old farmhouse on those long-gone Saturday nights seemed like a heaven I had left behind.

The fall of the year was wood-cutting time. Our trees were mostly red, white and black oak. There were no maples around there, and though some places had pine, there was none on our land. I liked to cut the red oak because it was easiest to handle. Hickory was mighty hard to split, but it made wonderful fuel and smelled great. We built rail fences, laid zig-zag—the way you seldom see them any more. It was considered extravagant to buy a lot of wire for fences when you had the material on your place for building your own

14

barriers, provided you weren't afraid to work and sweat a little.

We cut log chunks for our heating stove and split wood for the cook stove. This was all piled on our back porch where it was handy for Mother. It was my job to keep it piled up there and I still get a nice, warm glow, thinking back, to hear Mother compliment me as she looked at the wood pile and dried her hands on her apron.

There have been some milestones in my career as a clown —times when my spirits rose at the sound of applause or when I had been complimented by people in high places, and it was always the same thing: it was my mother standing at the kitchen door looking at the wood pile and telling me, "Well, you are a fine boy and you have done a good job."

We kept baby chicks behind the kitchen stove when they were first hatched, and we brought baby lambs into the house. Sis and I loved that, but what I liked best on our farm, next to my mother's cooking, was the pond. It was surrounded by willows at one end and at the other end it was deep enough to swim in. There were cattails in the shallow part and we could find watercress there, too. It was fed by a spring and a creek ran away from it in a lazy pattern all around over the farm. Our neighbor, George Wheeler, stocked that pond, so we could fish for bass, crappie and perch. I liked to shoot bullfrogs there with a rifle and in the fall when the pond flooded there would be good duck shooting. There were no game laws then. Wild geese stopped on our pond as they flew southward and we got some of them with a shotgun. Even my mother joined in and one day, I recall, she got three geese with one barrel. There were water moccasins on our place, but they never flourished because I kept after them. I'd sneak up quietly and shoot their heads off when they were on rocks or on the bank. None of us was ever bitten by these ornery critters, but they are mighty poisonous and mean-looking to boot.

In the winter, our pond would freeze to six or eight inches and we cut the ice. We used cant hooks and we sawed it in strips. Then we laid it within two feet of the inside of our ice-house walls which were double and made of pine. Between the piled-up ice and the walls was this two-foot space where we shoveled sawdust to make a good cushion of insulation. In the heat of the summer, the neighbors who had helped us cut and store the ice would come for their share and usually there was enough to outlast the hot weather. On Sundays we would freeze homemade ice cream. I remember how hard it was to turn the crank in the ice bucket when the cream was about done. It was crisp and flaky and not like the ice cream sold in stores.

My first real plow job came one spring when Dad decided to dig up the south pasture and try to raise a crop of corn. That job really broke me in the hard way because the soil was rocky and full of grubs. I had to cut out some of the roots and stumps with an axe. When I'd hit them, they'd bounce back like a punching bag and whip my legs. The land I liked to plow was beside the pond—good, rich, dark dirt with no rocks at all, and sometimes I'd find Indian arrowheads in that field.

Dan and Charlie were our horses. Dan was too chunky for a saddle, so I rode Charlie in a secondhand saddle that pitched forward because Charlie had a hump on his back. He was thin and tired, too, and I was ashamed to ride him to town. When I rode with other boys, I would always be last. I yearned for a nice, new saddle and fancy bridle and a fast horse.

Father bought a colt which was beautiful to look at, but he was wild and free and he aimed to stay that way. We never did manage to make a saddle horse out of him. Later on, I raised a calf and sold it for enough to send to a mail-order house for a Mead bike. That was in about 1913 or 1914 and I drove the wagon to town to pick it up. I opened the crate on the spot and there it was, all brown and shiny—one of the prettiest sights I ever saw. This way I could speed up our mail service by pedaling to town instead of waiting for the hack that came down our road from Houston.

Sis and I always were impatient for mail. You can't realize how much it can mean unless you've lived out on a farm back in the days before radio. The big day was always the one when *The Youth's Companion* arrived. Mother took a needlework magazine and Dad subscribed to *Successful Farming* and the *St. Louis Globe Democrat*. Our books at home, I suppose, were the usual thing—*Robinson Crusoe, Pilgrim's Progress* and Horatio Alger's, and, of course, the Bible.

My folks not only managed to finish paying Wheeler for the first eighty acres; they bought and paid for forty more and later on added another forty. They were quiet, efficient operators and while we lived simply, I don't remember that we ever really needed anything we couldn't have. Probably we always were in what even back then would be called a low-income bracket, but it never occurred to me that we were poor. There was no unemployment insurance, no farm subsidy, no old-age pension. And I'm sure that those things never bothered my father's mind. All he asked for was opportunity.

I've heard people who had been raised on farms do a lot of talking about the fun they had on Halloween, but where I lived we didn't make anything of it except jack-o-lanterns out of pumpkins. The spine-tingling event was the "shivaree." I remember the one at Lupton's farmhouse, which was set back in a grove. We cleaned our shotguns and put spare shells in our pockets and took along anything that would make noise and sneaked through the woods with the lanterns put out as we neared the place. Then at a signal somebody would lead

17

off and everything would pop loose. It was the craziest din I ever heard. Pretty soon, the newlyweds would appear—or at least the bridegroom would, and pass out cigars.

The really big thing down in that country was the Old Settlers' Reunion, held around the middle of August for three days. We used to pray for good weather, save our pennies, nickels and dimes and attend on the opening day and on the third and last day. We'd be brokenhearted if it was pouring rain because the folks wouldn't start, although Sis and I would have been willing to get soaking wet just to be there.

But if the weather was good, we'd get an early start. Mother would cook chicken in a box lunch. We'd take nubbins for the horses and we would dress up. Dad wore new overalls; Mother her best gingham dress and bonnet, and Sylvia a dress that Mother had likely just finished for her. I wore clean overalls and my ears and neck hurt where they had been scrubbed.

We jogged along in the farm wagon the four miles to Houston and our excitement mounted with every step old Charlie and Dan took. After we had unhitched the horses, we started to make the rounds. The layout was always the same —a merry-go-round run by a steam engine, two or three side shows and some eating stands and a platform or a flat farm wagon big enough for the free acts to perform on. I memorized the spiel the fellow had for the snake eater and I still remember it: "Men, women, ladies and gentlemen—right this-a-way to see Snakoid, the only man in the world that swallows them alive. He is just like you or I, but he eats them alive right before your eyes or we will give you your money back."

It was at this celebration that I saw my first motion picture—*The Great Train Robbery*—in what is called a "blacktop," a tent of black or dark blue canvas to prevent light from coming in during the daytime.

We bought confetti to throw at the girls and we bought

18

"singing" balloons, the kind that had wooden pegs at the end through which the air blew over a reed and made a kind of singing noise. Texas County was dry, but there was moonshine and Dad used to like to nip a little with our neighbor McKinney. The only disappointment in those wonderful occasions was having to leave before the balloon ascension. We had to start home before sundown in order to get our chores done. Sometimes, though, we would stop our horses outside of town and look back to see the daredevil on the swinging bar underneath the big inflated bag—watch breathless while he cut away and descended with a parachute.

It was at the schoolhouse picnic one summer afternoon that I saw an automobile for the very first time. There was a commotion down the road and Doc Blankenship drove right into the picnic grounds. It was an open car all trimmed in brass and it smelled of gasoline and made plenty of noise. The doctor wore goggles and gloves. He hauled all of us kids by turns, driving in a great circle on the picnic grounds, and when he took out onto the road again and started back to town, we stood and watched him out of sight and never said a word. Somehow it was sinking into us simple farm kids that something remarkable had happened to us which would never wear off, and that the world would never be quite the same for us any more.

There were other holidays and events worth recalling in my rural days, and Thanksgiving was one of the most important. We would trade visits with the Fishers each year. They had a boy named Earl and two daughters, which made a big day for my sister. The women prepared the dinner together while the men and boys went hunting. Earl and I had Stevens rifles, single-shot twenty-two caliber. I got to be a pretty good shot and we would spend most of Thanksgiving Day hunting squirrels and rabbits. We'd hunt all morning, eat a big dinner and go out again.

But Christmas was the champion event of the year and I can even remember one back in Kansas the year before we left for Missouri. We had a Christmas tree and Mother strung popcorn for it. The tree made the whole house smell wonderful. I got a drum among other things and Sis got a doll and a set of dishes. I won't forget a Christmas in Missouri when we didn't believe in Santa Claus any more. My father was working up a big surprise for us. He didn't know that his timetable was off and that he was a year too late. He had a red suit that my mother had made him, as well as some whiskers made out of rope.

We had wood stacked up on the back porch and we heard some of it tumble. That was the signal. Mother said, "I think it must be Santa out there." Sis and I said "No, it's not, it's Daddy." But she shushed us and we let Father carry it off as though we believed it. He brought me a blackboard with colored chalk which not only thrilled me, but proved to be my springboard into show business. The Christmas tree always was at the big double window on the south side of our house. My mother played carols on our old pump organ and made wonderful popcorn balls at holiday time. We had our own cane on the farm, and we used to take it to the mill where it would be ground and given back to us as molasses which Mother would make into German cookies that had our own walnuts and hickory nuts in them.

I started school soon after we moved to Missouri. It was a one-room frame school a mile and a quarter from our house. The neighbors up the road were a sizable family with six girls and one boy—the McKinneys. Sis and I would go to their farm and wait for the Wheeler kids, of which there were three, and then the twelve of us would all walk to school together, swinging our dinner buckets. In the winter, we walked through snow, sleet and rain, and sometimes the weather was so bad there was no school.

My favorite subject was geography. I loved to look at the maps and dream of someday visiting those places. We had eight grades in that schoolhouse and one teacher handled it all. I didn't quite finish the eighth grade, for they needed me on the farm that spring. Fortunately, one of our teachers encouraged my interest in drawing. I would be drawing pictures of trains or ships and feel a hunch somebody was watching me and turn around to find it was the teacher. He never scolded me, but instead told my dad, "That boy has talent; don't discourage him."

We were afraid of storms back in Missouri. Everybody who had ever lived in Kansas tornado country was storm conscious. We built a storm cellar on our farm in Missouri and when we'd see a black cloud with lightning in it, Mother would say: "Well, we'd better take to the cellar." If it was night, we'd take a lantern. Our home was lit with coal-oil chimney lamps, but we did not take them to the storm cellar. This refuge was about forty feet from the kitchen, it was built half underground and half on top with a dirt covering in the shape of a mound and a slanting door. We kept produce in there—a kraut barrel and apples and the like. One night when we were in the storm cellar, my dad peeked through the crack in the door to see how the sky looked and saw that a neighbor's barn was on fire from a bolt of lightning. Everybody in the neighborhood hurried over there, but it was too late to save the barn.

Sometimes we would go to the Airdrome, which was nothing but some benches facing a big white screen inside a galvanized iron enclosure and, at the back, a motion-picture machine that an operator turned with a hand crank. In the wintertime, there were movies in the D.A.R. Hall, but it was too hot there in the summer months. The heat in the hall wouldn't have been as bad as the mosquitoes in the Airdrome, but we were too thrilled by *The Perils of Pauline, The Trey*

21

of Hearts and *The Girl and the Game* to notice the bugs. I even enjoyed the lantern-slide advertisements.

Although Houston was our county seat, it had no railroad. Yet, on cold, clear nights we could hear an engine's long, drawn-out lament eighteen miles distant at Cabool. When this happened, my dad would get a far-away look in his eyes and square his jaw. We never talked about it, but we all knew there were plenty of times when he missed the railroad.

We went to that railroad once a year, in the autumn. Later we went twice because then we shipped dressed chickens, but at first we went just the one time to bring back the fertilizer. My daddy and the neighbors would get together and buy a carload and save money. It came to Cabool and it was up to the farmers to go there and get it.

It was quite a thrill to drive eighteen miles with horses and wagon. Mother would fry some chickens—fix up what my daddy called a "grub box" of homemade bread and pies. We would carry hay and grain enough for the trip which would begin at daylight. We would arrive in Cabool around one o'clock in the afternoon. It was crisp autumn by now. We sometimes would stay overnight at the livery barn, putting up the horses there and ourselves sleeping in a kind of bunkhouse. We took our own bedding. Other times, we would start back home before nightfall and camp near a creek. Dad would make coffee in a tin bucket—the best-tasting coffee I ever had—and we would sleep under the wagon. Sometimes we had to make two round trips. The fertilizer came in two-hundred-pound sacks and wasn't easy to handle.

When we got home again, the fields were plowed and ready for wheat drilling. The grain was dumped into the machine's bin-like container and the fertilizer was put in there too. Then the horses were started. The wheat drill cut through the soil, making little furrows while wheat and fertilizer fell into these furrows through a tube.

I was drilling wheat one autumn afternoon when the horses started to bolt. Almost at that instant, my sister yelled to me from the house and pointed to the road. I watched and saw a funny-looking wagon coming with four mules hitched to it. It was painted a dirty, scratched yellow. It had long poles on the side. I started for the house and stood by the road, gaping at this strange procession as one odd-looking wagon after another rolled by. I never had seen anything like this before. I had heard of circuses but this was my first. It was the Mighty Haag show, a famous small-time outfit in which the great dance-band cornetist, Harry James, grew up. His daddy was its band leader. They had an elephant and its feet were wrapped in gunnysacks. There was one camel and a cage with a bear in it. I hollered to a driver and asked him where they were going. "We're showin' in Yukon tonight," he said.

That night I rode my bicycle into Yukon and saw that show. They had only a small menagerie, but it had a tiger in it and under gasoline lamps I beheld my first clown, a little white-faced guy who belonged to the long-gone "talking clown" tradition. One of the acts was the buckboard kicking mule, and there were trained ponies and a girl contortionist, but no aerial acts. Yukon was nothing but a blacksmith shop and a general store—not a real town where you could expect a show to stop. Probably the Mighty Haag outfit was just doing a "quickie" as it headed south in a hurry to escape the cold weather.

But, insignificant as it was, I couldn't get it out of my mind. Then, wonder of wonders, I was in Houston two days later and saw a poster advertising that the great M. L. Clark and Sons Combined Shows was coming to town. This, too, was a small circus, but compared with the one I had seen it might have been as big as Barnum & Bailey. I sensed this from the advertising and determined to see it. My folks rarely said you can't do this or that. I was getting to be a big boy now,

23

and so long as I did my work they let me do about as I pleased.

I finished sowing the winter wheat and then rode my bike into Houston to watch that circus set up. Some distance from the show grounds, I could see the tents and I felt my blood begin to pound. The parade was soon in the streets and the music of the band thrilled me even more. The musicians wore red uniforms and they were followed by some mounted people and a couple of cages of animals. There was a zebra, the first I'd ever seen, and a steam calliope. I hurried back home to do the chores and return for the evening performance.

This show had electric lights. Out near the fence there was a light plant. They made their own juice and this fascinated me, although it was nothing but a little gasoline engine pecking away. The performance itself was in two rings. They had trapeze acts, cloud swings, a bucking mule and a couple of clowns. I was surprised when I came out because part of the circus had packed up and gone—the cook and dining equipment and the wild animal menagerie tent.

As I walked away I looked back and wondered where it had come from and where it was going. The farm seemed far away. Something that later caught fire in me was stirring that night. But I was a farm boy and school was starting and I had to go home.

Probably it would make a good story if I said that when I saw my first circus I immediately had a desire to be a clown. It wouldn't be true. Even when I finally took off after the red wagons, I never meant to be a clown. My ambition as a kid and as a young man and, even now, has been to be an artist.

That winter in Houston, after I had got a glimpse of the circus, marked the time when my mother encouraged my artistic leaning by spending twenty-five dollars for a correspondence course in cartooning. She had heard about the course and she had faith in my ambition so she sent for it—at a dollar a lesson—to the Landon School of Cartooning in Cleveland, Ohio.

They sent me drawing paper and pencils and I mailed them back what I did for them to criticize and send me the next lesson. About this same time, I got a book by Guy Lockwood with instructions on how to do a chalk-talk and this fascinated me. I went into town to the *Houston Republican* and bought a batch of flat newsprint sheets and had a carpenter build me an easel. I bought the book on how to do the chalk-talk and practiced hard.

There had lately been a time when the world of music had been given an outside chance at my native gifts. Mother played the violin as well as the piano, but for some reason she borrowed the instrument of a neighbor named Stephens when she decided to try my hand at it. Stephens was a good fiddler and his violin was a good one. Mother and he would play duets at musicals held in the farm homes from time to time. I remember the first violin lesson that came from a place called the U.S. School of Music. My mother paid her hard-earned money for that course too. The first lesson was positions, the second was how to draw the bow and the third was fingering. After that I gave it up and Stephens took his fiddle back where it belonged. I had made up my mind to be a cartoonist! At least, it was something I had a real feeling for.

My first appearance before an audience of any kind was at a pie supper in the schoolhouse. The entertainment usually consisted of the auctioneering of the pies (by my father), some music and recitations. I was pretty nervous. I had on my new dark suit and a bow tie I had learned to tie myself. Finally, I took a deep breath and said, "Ladies and gentlemen, I will now endeavor to entertain you with a few lightning sketches. For my first picture, I will draw my name." I was stiff as a board, but I began to get the feel of my audience as I turned the name picture into a face, then drew a column of figures

25

and turned that into a funny face. "Two in the water five minutes" turned out to be a couple of babies splashing in a tub. A moon became a sailboat when reversed, and I finished with a picture of Uncle Sam. There was applause after each effort and quite a nice send-off at the end. In the audience was a McKinney daughter who taught in a schoolhouse in a township four or five miles west of us. She asked me to appear as the feature attraction at a pie supper. Her father, she said, would drive me over in their buggy. For this trip I wore my dad's sheepskin-lined coat, mittens, earmuffs and felt boots. It was dark when we left and it was around zero. We took a trail through the woods and the buggy wheels crunched in the crusted snow. Myrtle McKinney had a big fire going in the schoolhouse when we arrived, but nobody came to the supper. The three of us sat around the stove and ate pie and then we drove home again. I played to nobody and that was the first and last show I ever had to call off.

Mother told me that Wagner, the artist, was coming as a feature of the Brown & White Lyceum circuit in the D.A.R. Hall. This man was the first real entertainer I ever paid much attention to. He did magic and caricatures and he was so clever that he discouraged me. Afterward, I was too bashful to go up and introduce myself to Wagner. Some of my pals lifted my spirits a bit at the soda fountain that night by assuring me that "Shucks, Tater, you're jest as good as that feller!" It was one of the biggest lies I ever heard, but it made me feel much better.

I was growing up fast now. At school, some of us boys began to experiment with chewing tobacco. We'd take a plug out in the woods, gnaw off a tiny bit of it and start spitting. One day, my mother said, "I hear you are chewing at school." I said, "Not exactly; we just nibble a little."

"Well," my wise mother replied, "Bert Wheeler chews and if you want to chew, I'll bring you a plug of tobacco next

26

time I go to town. Which kind do you want—Star Plug or Horse Shoe?"

I said I'd take the Horse Shoe and I felt pretty big. Sure enough, she brought me a plug next time she went shopping. She also built a roaring fire and told me to sit beside it and not spit on the floor. I was to use the ash container instead. She then said, "Now, don't just nibble at it; if you are going to chew, chew like a man. Take a big chew."

It wasn't long before the combination of hot stove and man-size chewing had me sick enough to want to die. I never chewed tobacco again. Mother was very tender with her sick son, and it was quite awhile before I tumbled to the fact that she had framed me.

The fair sex occupied my mind a good deal at this time, and I had the misfortune to pick a girl in Houston with competition in the shape of a tough guy who was said to carry a pistol. One Saturday night when I was in town, he and another boy asked me if I would go for a ride with them. I got off old Charlie and went with them, wondering what was up— scared to go and too proud not to. The tough kid stated the case very simply: "You ain't goin' with her any more. I am." Then he put his hand on his hip where I figured he carried the pistol, and I decided I couldn't whip both these guys and the gun to boot. So I promised not to go with the girl any more. I made myself a promise, too. And I kept it a week later when I met the fellow all alone. I stopped him now and did two things: I quickly said, "Well, how do you feel about it now that you ain't got your crowd with you?" and I hit him square in the nose.

It knocked him flat and cut his lip and bloodied his nose. The town marshal came and pinched us both and we wound up in jail. My father was in town that night and came down to the jailhouse. The fellow I'd fought had to pay $1.65 and so did I for disturbing the peace. My dad paid my fine and that was the end of it. He never said anything about the fight after that. The fellow I'd knocked down paid his fine and a week later the siren we'd fought over wasn't going with either of us. She had a brand new beau.

One of the prominent figures in Houston was the fellow who drank heavily and fought with a knife . . . a real tough mugg. One Saturday night, a couple of us farm kids saw a commotion in an alley. We edged up closer and saw the town marshal holding a gun on this tough character who had his knife on the officer's shoulder, threatening to stick it into his neck. Finally, the marshal shot the guy in the leg. When we saw the blaze of the 38-caliber, we ran. They carried the wounded man up the street and into the back of a store. We peeked in at a window and watched the doctor take the bullet out of his thigh. Then they took him to jail and he made a lot less trouble from then on.

We had a sort of neighborhood bully who lived a few miles from us and we never liked to have him show up at the pie suppers in the schoolhouse. He always was half loaded with moonshine when he came in and liquor made him meaner than he was naturally. One time during the auctioneering of the pies, we heard a commotion outside. Pretty soon the door burst open and this hell-roaring, drunken wild man stormed into the schoolroom. He had a long knife in his hand and began threatening people. One man tried to kick it out of his hand and was nicked in the shin. Eventually, three or four men sneaked up behind the drunk and grabbed him.

There never was any excitement on election days in Houston, for the county was so heavily Democratic that the Republicans amounted to very little voting strength. I remember the Wilson-Hughes campaign, for I used to draw Hughes in my chalk-talk. I would sketch a bunch of trees and when the picture was turned upside down they'd be the beard of the statesman. William Jennings Bryan had a good face to draw, too.

When we got into the war, I was too young to go, but some of the fellows I knew went to Waco, Texas, and sent back photographs that showed them in uniforms that fit badly. I got a job that spring in Blankenship's drugstore. It was operated by a man named Doc Haggard who had taken over Blankenship's practice and his store when Blankenship went to war. I was just a handy boy around the drugstore. I lived in a boardinghouse and hung around Freeland's Hotel in my spare time and listened to the traveling salesmen talking on the front porch. They seemed like great men of the world to me.

1917 was a year when a great restlessness was in me. I still expected to be drafted and I did not look forward to it with any pleasure. I helped weekends on the farm, but worked the rest of the time in the drugstore and tried to save a little money. I was promoted to the making of ice cream by Doc Haggard and I remember the hell he gave me the day I made the whole batch without putting in any vanilla. I worked up a small supply of cartoons, improved my chalk-talk act and at last, by springtime, decided the time had come to make the big break. I was going to Kansas City and get a job.

In the circus parade there is glory clean down
From the first spangled horse to the mule of the clown.

James Whitcomb Riley

CITY BOY

Kansas City! What a word that was in my childhood. Cabool and Houston and even Springfield were places
that you could visit in the course of a lifetime, maybe, but
Kansas City! And to take off for that great place and actually
live there was a mighty big deal.

The tough part of it was having to tell my folks, though
I guess they expected it. The work in Houston had made me
dissatisfied with the farm. It seemed so quiet and the same
things happened day after day after day.

I tried to soften the blow by saying that I was just going
to Kansas City to prospect a little—to see what I could find
and stay maybe only a few days. With this, I fooled nobody.
My dad had some years on him now and if I left home, they
would have to hire help.

But there wasn't any holding me. I had eighteen or
twenty dollars saved up. All my belongings for the trip I put
in my suitcase, went to Cabool on a beautiful spring day,
bought a ticket for Kansas City and waited in the depot for
the four-o'clock train going west.

This was a local that ran from Memphis to Springfield,

where I had to change. I slept in the daycoach and pulled into the great new depot at Kansas City a little after daybreak. I had no job and no place to live and not much money, but I stood in the most magnificent place I ever had seen. I was spellbound and stayed in it for a couple of hours—wandering around, gaping at the mammoth arch, listening to train callers, watching baggage men; having a cup of coffee and some breakfast in a Harvey restaurant, being fascinated by the news and cigar stand and most of all by the endless stream of people.

After soaking up all I could of this magic, I had one last ice-cream soda, picked up my cheap suitcase and walked out the front door. On the roof of a big building nearby was an electric sign turned on even in the daytime! It read: "Sweeney Auto School," and stated that it taught automobile mechanics.

I started up a steep hill, where now there is a memorial park, and came to the Park Hotel which I found to be too expensive for me. It was European plan, too, and I wanted to live where I could get my meals. The clerk sent me to a boardinghouse next door and right away I liked the old two-story frame with the two-seated swing in the front yard. A jolly, heavy-set woman answered my ring and sold me a room for five dollars a week. I shared the room with another boy, a blond, chunky, farm-like and friendly fellow from Texas who was taking the course at Sweeney's. We slept in a double bed. My roommate was quiet and studious and we got on well together.

Almost everything I did those first few days in the big city has stuck in my memory. Instead of being annoyed by the train smoke and the noise of the steam and the ringing of the bells and the warm, sickening odor that came from the nearby Wilson Packing House when the wind was right for it, I thrilled to these sights and sounds and smells. We sat out in the yard in the swing and watched the other boarders coming home. The table the landlady set was really something special and we ate all we could hold.

That night, I was drawn back to the railroad station as if by a magnet. I spent an hour just standing on a bridge, watching the trains going in and out, the railway express being handled, the hacks and the people. The main part of Kansas City lies back of the depot and some distance away, so I took a walk. The street I'd selected was occupied mostly by cheap stores and pawnshops, and I wondered if I would be handing my watch across the counter of one of these establishments before I could get a job. Tired at last, I drank some lemonade and went back to the boardinghouse and to bed.

Next morning, I took my roll of cartoons under my arm and headed for the main part of town. I took a streetcar to avoid getting lost and when we stopped at a corner where the Globe Theatre was, I got off. That theatre had an electric sign that ran day and night and it impressed me considerably. I asked for the *Kansas City Star,* but when I learned it was a good many blocks away, I went to the *Journal* instead. It was closer. I had no trouble getting to see the managing editor. He reared back in a swivel chair while I explained that I had finished my course in the Landon School of Cartooning and would like to show him my samples.

He looked them over and said, "Now, we don't have any job for a cartoonist, but I sort of like this picture and if it is all right with you I'll keep it for a while. I may run it and I may not. You can come back and get it any time you like."

I left the cartoon and I was so thrilled I still remember the details of the drawing. It was entitled "How People Will Live in the Future" and it depicted a house swung under a cigar-shaped balloon, probably influenced by pictures of the German zeppelins. A woman was hanging her washing and the wind was whipping it, and kids played on a porch while the old man sat smoking. A cat lay asleep on the front steps.

33

I left the cartoon with the newspaperman and never did go back for it. I doubt if it ever saw print; at least I never saw it, although the possibility of its appearance made a subscriber out of me for several weeks.

At the lower end of Grand Avenue, I came to the bigger paper—the *Star,* and the country boy was surprised again to be taken to the editor without having to wade through a battery of secretaries or having to sit around and wait for an hour or so. He was a kindly man who explained that they needed only one cartoonist and that job was filled by the fellow who drew a strip called "The Intellectual Pup." I then told him that if they couldn't take me on as a cartoonist, they might hire me in some other capacity—so I'd be handy if anything happened to their artist. I was sent to see the foreman of the pressroom in the basement. He had nothing for me, so I became discouraged and left the building. Across the street was a fruit stand where I bought a coconut, cracked it on the sidewalk and ate it all. Then I saw what I took to be the biggest orange I ever had seen. It was a grapefruit, but I didn't know it. I bought one and took it back to my room and tried to eat it, inner skin and all. The bitter, sour taste convinced me that I had made a mistake; the fruit wasn't fit to eat. It wasn't until later that I saw a fellow eating grapefruit with a spoon in a restaurant.

My mind was now on the fact that I needed a job. Everyone else in the place was busy and I felt out of it. The promising young cartoonist had swung and missed both times at bat in this town and he didn't know of anywhere else that might use his talents. I made up my mind to go out and get some kind of a job. I still had a few dollars in my pocket and the idea of returning to Houston and the farm with my tail between my legs didn't appeal to me in the least.

At the warehouse of the International Harvester Company, I missed again; they didn't need men there. Next I came to a place called the Meridian Creamery Co. I watched them at the loading platform—rolling cans off express cars and into trucks. It was noisy and busy as hell and there was spilt milk on the floor and water being sloshed around. A tall, nice-looking guy with a pencil over his ear and a board under his arm seemed to be in charge, so I asked him for a job. "This work is kind of heavy; do you think you can lift these cans?" he asked. "I can do it. I'm a farm boy! I've pitched hay!" I answered in a rush of words. "All right, son, you can come to work at noon. But you have to have white overalls, white jacket and white cap and you have to furnish them yourself. The pay is twenty-one bucks a week."

I felt so good that I didn't mind having to spend $2.50 for the white outfit. I bought the stuff on Main Street, hurried back to the boardinghouse for lunch and reported for work at the creamery. The work was hard, but I liked it well enough, and the boss was a nice guy. I helped roll the heavy cans off the cars, knock off the lids with a hammer, dump them as soon as the foreman had taken his samples for the testing room, wash the cans with steam pressure and hot water and then throw the empties onto the chute. Later they put me into the butter room where I learned to cut the butter with a wire knife that sliced out twelve separate pounds when you got the hang of it. I liked the cutting room because seven or eight girls worked in there and I could amuse them by drawing cartoons. One little redhead would pretend to be sore and would throw butter at me when I'd get fresh, but she was the one who wrote to me long after I'd left town. At night, after the girls went home, the foreman and I had to clean the place with hose and hot water, running it all over the ceilings, the paddles, tables and floor. A cold-water rinse followed until finally the whole place was spotless.

One day in the middle of the summer, I took stock of myself and decided that the creamery wasn't helping me get

35

any closer to a career as a cartoonist; so I got a job in a sign shop where I made wood frames, covered them with zinc and put on a coat of primer. The only actual painting I got to do, though, was atop a scaffold with a painter who let me fill in around the lettering. Pretty soon, we got to working up high and took on a big wall near the roof of the packing company. The painter had a habit of shaking the scaffold or swinging the gallery-like rigging on which we worked our way up and down the wall. Sometimes the whole caboodle would swing out and I would have to grab a rope to hang on, but this scared me so much that my hand would shake and I could hardly do the painting. My lunch hour was ruined every day by guys from the packing plant who came out to eat with us and who were covered with a red powder that I was pretty sure was blood. This nauseated me and so did the sight of watching them shovel bones.

The wife of the sign boss sensed that I was unhappy in my job. She spent some time asking me about my girl back home and told me how fine it would be when I'd get to be a union sign painter and have my wife with me in Kansas City. By this time, the weather was so hot that the paint bubbled on the walls and the roof tar stuck to my shoes, and I quit that job.

On my way back to the boardinghouse, I passed a place called Columbia Steel Tank Co. I walked in, told somebody I was handy with paint and they hired me. They gave me a set of brushes, paints, maul and pounce (stencil) pattern. The only trouble was that I never had painted a sign in my life and the boss soon knew it. He took me off that assignment and put me to work with a sign painter who saw that I couldn't do lettering. I wound up painting the insides of tank cars where the air was stifling. In three days I had painter's colic from inhaling lead and had to stop work.

A little worried at the way I was jumping around from

job to job, but determined to make my own way, I next took a job in a lumber yard. When the boss asked if I could drive a truck I said yes. I had driven Wheeler's little pick-up in the fields, but this was a big one with a load of lumber and I hadn't reckoned with the traffic problem. I got it out of the yard all right and onto the street, but by the time I had driven to the corner of 18th and Main, I had created a traffic jam that was a pip. The cop yelled, "Where the hell you going?" and asked me if I ever had driven a truck. I said no, so we had to haul the truck to one side and send for a guy to come and get it. The lumber-yard superintendent was good and sore, but he didn't fire me. He put me to stacking. I recollect that I didn't stay there long either.

In all these places I would make between eighteen and twenty-one dollars a week, not more. It was autumn of 1918 and I was up for the draft. If the war had lasted another month I'd have been in. By then I was employed by the Western Show Property Exchange, a novelty jobber, dealing in the cheap flashy stuff people try to win on carnival midways. My job was painting plaster kewpie dolls. Most of the other painters were girls. We were paid six cents for each small doll and eight for the bigger ones. I did pretty well and by Christmas time I had saved about fifty bucks plus the railroad fare to make a trip home. I had been sending post cards and letters, but Kansas City was a magic place that needed telling about in person. I wanted to go home and brag a little and, anyhow, I missed the folks.

I still had the same cardboard suitcase, but I now wore Kansas City-bought clothes and I had packages for all the family. They met me with the wagon at Houston and we headed for the farm. It surprised me by looking so much smaller. It was quiet and lonely and sort of dismal, too, I thought then. Within the short space of time I had spent in the big city I had lost the farm forever. But Christmas was wonderful with the family and I had a fine visit before returning to Kansas City after the first of the year.

The Western Show Property Exchange was owned and operated by Doc Grubbs, an old medicine showman. It handled, in addition to the kewpie dolls and other "prize" merchandise, gambling wheels, banners; secondhand stuff, too, that could be repaired and refurbished for sale again. When I returned there in the winter of 1919, I was put to work on dolls that were made to be thrown at by midway customers armed with baseballs. What the customers never knew was that while the dolls all looked alike, they wouldn't all fall over from the same impact because some were filled with cotton and some with sand.

I had to leave this job a second time because I caught influenza and ran a high fever and thought I was going to die. People did die—thousands of them—from that virulent form of flu, and I decided that if it happened to me it would happen at home. I was delirious on the way home, but my folks met me and Mother put me to bed and warmed me and called the doctor. Soon after that, Doc Haggard joined the ranks of the heroic medical men who wore themselves out in that epidemic and died of the bug they were fighting. I was able to move around again, on wobbly legs, after three weeks.

Returning to the city, I helped a tall, blond, thin fellow named Don with the painting of side-show banners—the pictorials that describe the freaks and the wonders on the midways in front of the side-show tents. Don was an accomplished scenic painter and we got to like each other.

One day I bought a secondhand stage drop from that place, took it back to the boardinghouse and hung it in my room. It was the size of a side-show platform backdrop and too small for any theatre stage, but I did not realize it. I wanted to use it as a background for my chalk-talk which I had started to practice up on again. I drew a fancy easel and

38

took the plans to a plumber who built it for me out of brass. I bought some green velvet with gold fringe on the bottom and rigged it on the easel so that it worked like a little stage curtain. When I was ready to start the act, I would draw a string and the curtain would part, revealing the blank paper. I'd ask the boarders in to watch me draw and I got to feeling my oats because nobody else there was in show business. To tell the truth, neither was I, but still my mind was on it increasingly, and I told myself it was simply a matter of breaking in.

I next entered a theatre amateur contest and proudly took my backdrop with me. The stagehands didn't laugh at me, but anybody could see that my "scenery" was too small for any stage. They masked it in from the sides for me. I won first prize in that contest—three dollars. Then I started to experiment with makeup, using some Stein's cream and a putty nose as I had seen burlesque comedians do. I attended shows regularly at the Gaiety and the Globe theatres and sometimes went to Loew's and the Orpheum to watch Fatty Arbuckle and Charlie Chaplin, Ben Turpin, Chester Conklin and other funny men. It occurred to me that I might combine my chalk-talk with some clowning and possibly change to pantomime.

One afternoon, rummaging around in Doc Grubbs' place, I found a box with a trapeze bar and crane. There were no guylines but I bought it anyhow, for three dollars. I lugged it home to the boardinghouse, but I put it away, since without guywires, it couldn't be rigged.

One day in the early spring, a fellow named Zieger who owned a small carnival dropped by and asked Doc Grubbs to loan him a painter. That is how I got my first job with a show—with Zieger's United Shows at the winter quarters in Weston, Missouri, where I painted the merry-go-round. The show property was in an abandoned brewery and it was about ready to roll. The word UNITED in Zieger's title was misleading. I don't know how it could have been much smaller *before* it was "united," for it operated as a two-car show. They loaded the merry-go-round, concession tents and three side shows and whatever else they had in the way of equipment into two baggage cars, and rented local horses and wagons to haul these from the railroad yards to the show grounds wherever they exhibited. Zieger asked me to go with the show and I fell for it.

In the time it takes to wink an eye, I was in charge of one of the side shows—I put up the tent, sold tickets and managed the thing, and it was called "Spidora." This was an illusion presentation in which it appeared that a living girl's head rested on top of a pedestal and that the girl had no body at all. Of course this was a mirror trick and I became very much aware that this pretty, dark-haired girl had nothing missing at all. But she was going with another carnival guy and it appeared unlikely that I would get to know her. This, coupled with the fact that one morning I felt an itching on my neck and reached up and picked off a louse, made me decide to leave this little show. I never had seen a louse before but I felt I could do without their companionship.

I went back to Kansas City and got a job in a drugstore for sixteen dollars a week. It was less than I had been making at the Western Show Property Exchange, but more than I got with the carnival. Anyhow, the show exchange work petered out in the summer months after the shows it served had taken to the road, and so I figured I would take almost any job for the time being. I floated through a good many jobs in a few years' time in Kansas City, but I always kept working at something.

People who see my tramp clown routines often conclude that I am probably the laziest fellow in the world. Out of character, I never got the hang of being idle. I was brought up on a farm where everybody worked and I've worked ever since, one place and another. I am uneasy if I am not employed at something.

The Sweringer Drugstore was near 18th and Indiana, if I remember rightly, and I worked the soda fountain, swept out the place and was left in charge once a day when the boss went to the bank. That usually was the signal for me to get into the candy case or make myself a fancy sundae with a lot of nuts on it. I still lived in a boardinghouse near the depot, but shortened the long distance to work by buying a second-hand bicycle. Sweringer and I got along well until the day John Robinson's Circus came to town and I was late for work after watching this big show unload and set up and parade. I told my boss the truth, but he was sore as a wet hen and though he did not fire me, our relationship worsened and pretty soon I was unemployed once more.

I had attended the Robinson Circus performance, which far surpassed anything I had ever dreamed of. There was some excitement when a girl fell from an iron-jaw rigging while spinning and hanging on with her teeth. They carried her out quickly. The band changed tempo and new acts came in and the show went along as though nothing had happened. I never did find out how badly she was hurt. A fellow seated next to me said, "If you think *this* is a big circus, go to see Sells-Floto and then if you think you've seen everything, take in the Ringling Brothers and Barnum & Bailey Circus when it comes to town. It travels on a hundred railroad cars!"

Of course I didn't believe him. I was an outsider then and knew nothing about the sizes of various shows. Later I found that while the public can be made to believe almost any fabrication in the amusement business, it seldom will accept the plain and simple truth.

After I saw the Robinson show, I got to thinking more and more about the trapeze rigging I had put away in a box in my room. The falling of the circus girl under John Robin-

41

son's big top didn't slow my enthusiasm, but I still had no guylines and I did not know how to hang the stuff alone. Later on I saw the Sells-Floto Circus, which was a fine, big show; but when the Ringling Brothers and Barnum & Bailey outfit hit town, I could hardly believe the size of it. I made a mental apology right then to the fellow I had thought was lying when he told me this tremendous thing needed a hundred railroad cars to move it from town to town. Moreover, I had a chance to count the cars and prove it. The show traveled on four separate trains and looked like a big town. There was a blacksmith shop and big cook and dining tents and a barber-shop tent and I could see a man delivering mail like a regular postman, and there were electric-light plants and water wagons—it was a sight I'll never forget. When the Sells-Floto Circus was in town, I had asked a man for a job with it and had been turned down. Now, unemployed and unable to spare seventy-five cents for a ticket to see this biggest of circuses, I was too awed by its magnitude to ask for work.

But I was nearly broke now and so was my roommate who had finished his course at the auto school and needed to start for Texas where he had a job lined up in a garage. We decided to head for the harvest fields where the rumor was that pay was five dollars a day. My buddy and I did not want to write home for money or let our folks know we were running so low. We pooled our resources and found we had enough to get us to Strong City, Kansas.

We got off the train and walked over to what looked like a couple of farmers and said: "Well, here we are—ready to work the wheat." They laughed and said it was too green to cut for two or three weeks yet. But they told us there was work there for us if we wanted it. My pal got a job riding a team that pulled a hayrack loaded with sewer pipe, but I had no job and was feeling blue. I stopped an old farmer in front of the bank and asked him if he could use a hired hand. He said yes and I got into his car. They were baling alfalfa at his place and I went to work alongside a big colored man, but trying to keep pace with him wore me out. I was soft from inside work and no work at all and after another day of it I had to quit.

My friend finished his job and we went to Kiowa, for we had heard they were cutting wheat down near the Oklahoma border. The minute we stepped off the train we were swamped. The farmers were grabbing everyone in sight. In no time at all, we were in a car and heading for a farm. They supplied us with overalls, straw hat and pitchfork, and paid five dollars a day. This work was hard, but after a week or so the man's crop was safe and the job was done.

The farmer tried to persuade us to join a threshing crew that would keep us working clean up into Nebraska and for several weeks, but I looked out at the machine and the mountainous cloud of dust the threshers were working in. I decided the job wasn't for me, but the Texan elected to try it. I lost track of him after that, and I can't remember his name, but if he ever reads this I wish he would come to see me the next time the circus plays Texas or wherever he is now.

The farmer got my check cashed for me in town. It was thirty dollars and more than enough to get me back to Kansas City.

When I returned, I had a letter that pleased me very much. I received an offer to play the Old Settlers' Reunion back home—and for pay! I would go back as a real professional this time and do the cartoon act and clown a little on the side.

I bought a misfit red coat and some funny-looking pants in a junky secondhand store, gathered up my drawing board, easel and chalk, and my cardboard suitcase, and set out for home.

The trapeze couple was on the bill again that summer

and we shared the same dressing tent. They liked my work, but thought I should do the cartoon act in a nice-looking suit instead of in a disreputable-looking clown costume.

I'll never forget when I first stepped out on the platform of that Old Settlers' Reunion. There was red, white and blue bunting in all directions and the familiar sounds and smells of the open-air carnival. The band was playing "Has Anybody Here Seen Kelly?"

Best of all, my mother and dad and sis and Jessie McKinney were in the front row. After the act was over, we made the rounds of the rides and shows and games and refreshment stands and I slept once more in my old room with the quiet night sounds that had so long been absent from my living—the bark of my old dog, the chirping of crickets, the croak of bullfrogs, the screech of an owl and occasionally the roar of a motor as an automobile burned up the pike to Houston. The next two nights I stayed at the hotel in Houston, for I was a professional entertainer now and felt that I should live in the town where the show was.

They paid me thirty dollars for three days and I did nine shows. The first write-up I ever received for clowning and cartooning appeared in the *Herald* and I still remember it by heart after all these years. It said: "Emmett Kelly, who was raised on a farm out in Ozark School District, came back to his hometown to do his cartoon act at the Reunion. He proved to be the best entertainer we had on the bill, considering what we paid him."

Back in Kansas City, I went at once to a booking agency and told him about my act. "We can't book you," he said. "There isn't any work this time of year for that kind of an act."

"All right," I said, "I have an idea. Let me draw pictures and sell them."

The idea appealed to this fellow, so he sent me to a celebration in Marsaline, Missouri, where I worked the street as a clown in the morning and set up my "studio" in the afternoon. My clown makeup was the "silly kid" type, with a white wig, white shirt, baggy short pants and comedy suspenders. I rented a room in a hotel and dressed there. The caricatures and sketches I drew of people—mostly kids whose parents wanted to park them somewhere to get rid of them for a few minutes—were sold for twenty-five cents each and it proved to be a hard, slow way to make money. But the thing that decided me against staying longer than one day on that job was the firecrackers. Kids would follow me while I clowned the streets in the morning and toss firecrackers and lighted cigarettes in the back of my shirt, which was purposely ragged and open all the way. I learned a few years later that one of the days the circus dreads most is Fourth of July, because in some towns hoodlums like to throw firecrackers under the feet of elephants. It can start a stampede, and that day on the streets of Marsaline I knew exactly how the elephants feel about it.

On the train, going back to Kansas City, I picked up a discarded *Billboard* magazine and read all the circus and carnival news I could soak up. It was only midsummer and I was out of work, and although I longed to be really in show business, I didn't know how to get started. I wouldn't have been able to sleep a wink on that train if I could have looked into the future, because in no time at all I was in show business up to my ears.

The Frisco Exposition Shows came to Kansas City and set up for one week on the location where I had seen the circuses. This was a forty-car carnival with a dog and pony show as one of its midway attractions. Andy Carson and Dave Lackman owned this outfit, and Mrs. Lackman operated the dog and pony circus. I went to her and told her about my cartoon act and she agreed to try me out. I decided to work in

45

clown makeup and she liked the act. I was put to work at a salary of twenty dollars a week and told to dress with an elderly man who was the show's one and only clown. I made up in whiteface, too, and did the chalk act. One of my stunts was to draw the old man, using him as a nervous and curious model who kept saying: "Does it look like me? Does it look like me?" I kept assuring him that it did, and when finally I turned it around so that he and the crowd could see the picture of a jackass, it brought a good laugh.

When I told Irene Lackman about my trapeze act she said I could put it in, but at no advance in salary. Considering the fact that I never had done any trapeze work at all, this seemed reasonable to me. Anyhow, I had a plumber complete my trapeze equipment and I rigged it, but I did not attempt a public appearance until I had mastered some simple tricks. I taught myself to circle the bar, do an ankle-drop and to hang by my hocks. The tent was so low I could almost touch the ground when I hung upside down. Then I got myself a set of red tights and a red gym shirt and I did the act, wearing clown makeup. I got away with it well enough, but I'm sure I didn't give the trained dogs and ponies much competition.

When the Frisco Shows were playing Pawhauska, Oklahoma, in came a good-sized circus named Yankee Robinson. This wasn't John Robinson's Circus that I had seen in Kansas City. Yankee Robinson was a showman who had been the first circus partner of the Ringling Brothers many years before. Somehow a Missourian named Fred Buchanan had acquired the title for his circus. I decided to try to get a job with a real circus.

Now I had an address. I told Frank Miller, the equestrian director and head of performing personnel for Yankee Robinson, that I was clowning and doing trapeze in the carnival's dog and pony show. He sent me to see Buchanan. The show's owner said that the tour was nearly over. "We have only two more weeks to go," he said, "but if you will write me a letter this winter to Lancaster, Missouri, I will probably hire you."

The circus left town, and at the end of the week our carnival shoved off also to play a stand in Tulsa, Oklahoma, where a big storm blew down all our tents. I sat out the storm in a wagon, which was all right, but the fact that I did not help with the tents afterward caused some resentment on the part of the carnival labor. I mentioned this to Mrs. Lackman and she told the complainers that I was a performer and not required to pitch in and help with the heavy work. Moreover, she explained, I was an artist and must take care of my hands. I took a quick look at my big, calloused "artist's" hands and shoved them into my pocket where nobody could see them.

I closed with this show the next week in Fort Worth. Back of the courthouse was an old dwelling with a sign in the window reading "Board and Room for $7." That was exactly the amount of money I had. I gave the landlady my money and sat down to wait for dinner. Soon a bunch of working men dashed into the house, ran upstairs and splashed water on themselves and returned to stand at the top of the stairs that led to the dining room in the basement. A rope was stretched across the top of the stairs. When the landlady rang the bell, the rope was thrown off and the men stampeded to the table. That woman set a beautiful table—loaded with roasts, mashed potatoes, pies and condiments galore. The men loaded their plates and ate fast without talking. I was mannerly and modest and kept saying, "Please pass the potatoes and please pass this-and-that" and sometimes they'd hand me a plate without even looking. I soon learned about the "boardinghouse reach" and that I would have to fend for myself in that company.

These roughnecks became my friends and later helped me get a job at the refinery where they worked. This was

47

after I had tried to work at a tombstone-cutting establishment where, because I had to have work, I assured the man that I could do any of the work if I could just get used to the tools. They gave me a chisel and hammer and set me to drilling and splitting big chunks of granite and they paid me about twenty bucks a week. They weren't sore when I quit to work with the oil men, and on the refinery job I got five dollars a day.

There, I helped dig ditches and lay pipe. It was a filthy job and I soon found that I couldn't keep clean. Once when we moved to Weatherford, Texas, to rig a pipe into an empty tank, another boy and I were supposed to steady a four-inch pipe that was being lowered inside that place from the top almost to the bottom. The place was empty and dark and rusty and the pipe was heavy and swinging from the rope with which they were lowering it, and I was scared to death. So was the other boy. The fellow lowering the pipe let it get away from him and it came down, missing us by inches.

We went outside and at that point they needed another man to go up on top of the tank and lower the pipe. There was one rickety ladder for this job and I soon regretted ever having told anyone in that gang that I had done trapeze work. "Let Kelly go up with the rope—he's a trapeze performer and won't mind the height!" somebody hollered.

I was stuck with it. They handed me a wrench that must have weighed ten pounds and I went up to the top to try to work the bolts loose on the intake plate. They were rusted and wouldn't budge. Meanwhile, the ladder would shake until I almost fainted with fright and somebody down below would yell, "Don't worry; you won't fall! Trapeze performers don't mind being up in the air thataway!"

At that moment I hated those guys, but I soon saw the comedy in it and they didn't razz me too much when I came down without getting the bolts off, or when I quit to go back to Kansas City soon after.

It was late in November when I returned to the big town, and I needed a job. I was walking down the street one morning and saw a sign that read: "Adv. Film Company." I wondered what it meant and if they could use a cartoonist. I went to the three-room layout on the third floor, consisting of an office up front, a workroom and a darkroom. The boss was named Whitcomb and I tackled him. "Not a bad idea," he said. "Have you got any samples? There is an outside chance we could use some cartooning."

Whitcomb liked my samples enough to put me on at twenty dollars a week. He rigged me out with drawing board, inks, scissors, etc. and set me to work next to a showcard writer. And there in that little plant was where my tramp clown character was born.

He came gradually, as a forlorn and melancholy little hobo who always got the short end of the stick and never had any good luck at all, but who never lost hope and just kept on trying.

That is the kind of clown I later became in the circus. Of course at that time I had no idea of making a career out of clowning. I was either a trapeze artist or a cartoon artist, and I did not see myself as a clown at all. Little did I realize that some years later, when I was told that I would have to start clowning or else, a sad little character who had been born on my drawing board in motion-picture advertising in Kansas City would nudge my mind gently and guide my hand and start to lead me.

> Clowns are pegs, used to hang circuses on.
>
> *Phineas T. Barnum*

FIRST OF MAY

I was happy in that cartoon job. It was just what I had been wanting to do. If I hadn't had a taste of trouping, I am sure I would have been satisfied to stay in that work exclusively. In another part of town, out on Troost Avenue, another young cartoonist was working whom I didn't meet until years later. His name was Walt Disney.

At the film company, I labored on animated figures which we cut out of paper and jointed so that they could be made to move while the photographer filmed each separate position. If the head was a profile, I would have to make five layouts. To make a face laugh, I'd have to work out three or four separate mouths. The best advertisement I ever drew and animated was for Sewell's Paints. It showed a little fellow with a bucket and brush coming out on a scaffold and going to work just as I had done on the packing-house wall. I spent too much of my pay attending the movie theatres where my film advertisements ran, but whenever the audience laughed at one of my cartoons, I'd be proud as a movie star at the premiere of his own picture.

I had remembered to write to the Yankee Robinson Cir-

51

cus that winter, and they mailed me a contract (with the name of the show changed to Howe's Great London Circus) for the coming tour. Now I had a real problem, for I not only enjoyed the work at the Adagram Film Company, but I hated to tell Mr. Whitcomb that I was leaving for the road.

So I put it off until the Saturday before the Monday when I would have to show up at circus winter quarters. On that day, just as I was getting up nerve enough to go to the front office, the boss sent for me. "Emmett, we've been watching you," said Whitcomb, "and we're very proud of your work. We're getting out a catalogue for a customer and we want you to think up a good cover for it and make the drawing."

I squirmed inwardly. "And I have some good news for you, Emmett," he added. "We are going to raise your salary to twenty-five dollars a week."

Now I really was in a pickle, for this was the exact sum I had been offered by the circus. Finally, after an embarrassing pause that was agony to me as I listened to the tick of the office clock, I said: "I'd like to do it, Mr. Whitcomb, and I'm tickled to death that you like my work, but I have signed a contract to go with a circus."

Whitcomb jumped forward in his chair. "A circus!"

"Yes, because I am a trapeze performer."

I thought he was going to faint. "Are you kidding?" he stammered.

"No, I'm a trapeze performer. I was with Irene Lackman's dog and pony show."

"Well," said the boss, "I'll swear this is something for the book. You didn't tell anybody."

I explained to him how I had learned the hard way to keep my mouth shut about trapeze work after my experience on top of the oil tank. Whitcomb laughed and said: "Now, wait a minute. How many weeks do you get with that circus?"

I told him I guessed about thirty, and that while the pay wasn't any higher than he was going to give me, I would get my board and sleeping quarters with the show.

"I don't think this will turn out to be very profitable for you, considering the winter lay-off," he argued, "but I won't try to stop you and I wish you luck." He put out his hand. That afternoon I was paid off, and the next morning I was on my way to the first real circus that ever hired me.

The circus wintered on a farm at Granger, connecting by traction line with the larger town of Lancaster. I got off the train and there stood a small man, older than I, who was looking me over. "Are you going with the circus?" he asked. When I told him I was "with it," he said: "My name is Lloyd Center and I do a ring act."

I told him what I did and asked him where I would find the boss. "I'll take you to him," Center offered. "Are you a First-of-May?" Now, a "First-of-May" is what circus people call a new trouper. The name comes from the fact that all the shows except the ones wintering in the Deep South or the warm states of the West begin their touring season on or about that date.

The manager of the show was Dan Odum. Odum had all the outward appearance of a showman. He gave the impression of height without being tall and he was built as if he might be able to take care of himself in a rough-and-tumble. He had a sense of humor, but I seldom saw it at work. Mostly, he was all business. He had a rough show and he knew how to handle it. On this first meeting, he looked me over quickly as if to size me up and with no more than ten words sent me to see the train porter.

Lloyd Center stayed with me and wised me up. All I needed to know to keep from sounding too green around my first circus I learned from him. I was amazed when they told me that the opening stand would be Albuquerque, New Mex-

ico. Our outfit was making one of the longest jumps in all circus history. These were the days of bitter competition among
circuses, and Howe's Great London Circus was going all that
distance to get into the West and fight the Al. G. Barnes show.

It turned out to be a fight we did not win, for the Barnes
outfit was owned by one of the brightest, far-sighted showmen
of this generation who had an unusual circus that featured
nothing but animals. He didn't have an acrobatic act or an
aerial number in the whole show—nothing but animals, and
wonderful novelties such as a lion act that finished with a
noble-looking old male with his woman trainer being hoisted
on a platform right out of the steel arena and up into the top
of the tent while fireworks shot off from the four sides of the
platform. Barnes was also the first showman to have a hippopotamus out of its cage and waddling around the hippodrome
track. The two circuses got in each other's path and tried to
beat each other to the same towns, until we got the worst of
it and eventually turned away into less competitive territory.

But all that was in the middle of the tour. To get back
to my first day with my first circus—I was thrilled with the
loading of the show, all newly painted and ready for the road.
We had over a hundred head of horses, seven elephants, some
camels, a lot of cages, and we traveled on twenty-five railroad
cars. The train's boss porter took me into a sleeping car and
showed me a berth with two names on a card tacked to it.
One of the names was mine. "Everybody has to double up on
this show," the porter explained.

I told him I didn't like it. "You don't have to bawl me
out," he replied. "Go see Mister Odum, he's the boss."

Wisely, I figured that this day, when the show was loading and pulling out of town, was no time to bother the manager about a minor problem. There was nothing to do but
sleep where they'd put me for the first night anyhow.

Circuses always have been marvels of space economy and

54

to this very day build their flatcars seventy-two feet long, which is fourteen feet longer than a railroad-system flat. These carry the wagons. Circuses pay freight rates per car, and so the longer the cars the better break the show gets. In the old days, the personnel all slept two in a berth, except for a few executives and featured acts, and in the workingmen's cars the berths were built three-high so that a hundred men could be crowded into a single sleeping car. Some of the smaller shows had no sleeping accommodations whatever for the workingmen and they slept under the wagons on the flatcars.

The fellow I bunked with that first night said he didn't care which side he slept on, so I picked the inside. There was no room in the berth for clothing, and I was mad because I had to fold my pants and park them under the pillow. We were in a tier of berths so low that I couldn't look out a window and watch the scenery.

That was a sleepless night. Next day, when the circus stopped to water and feed the animals and set up the cookhouse for a few hours to feed the people, I spoke to Dan Odum about the sleeping problem and he let me bunk with my friend, Lloyd Center.

Because we stopped once every twenty-four hours at predetermined points for watering, the trip to the opening stand took three days. The morning we arrived in Albuquerque was the windiest I had ever seen. It was almost impossible to get the tents into the air, but at last we were ready for rehearsal.

Frank Miller was equestrian director. He was a light-complected, slight man—all wire and grace, especially in the saddle. His blue eyes were kindly and though he took no foolishness from a horse, I never saw him abuse one. Miller was from old Missouri stock and "weaned on a Morgan mare," as some of the hoss fraternity often bragged. Sometimes the public calls this man the ringmaster, but he isn't. A ringmaster stands in the center of a ring of trained horses; a circus equestrian director is in charge of the whole performance and of all performing personnel.

The performers all assembled in the big top and Miller called off the names. My contract called for me to do trapeze work and to double in clowning, which meant that the aerial work was my principal job and the clowning was secondary. In addition, I was to "make oneself generally useful." This was the joker in the contract; all circuses had it in those days. To make oneself generally useful meant everything from riding parade to helping put up canvas, erect the seats, load trunks and do whatever had to be done during a shortage of help.

The toughest part of the rehearsal for me was the Garland Entry. This was a horseback drill in which eighteen riders, carrying flower garlands entwined on springy sticks about ten feet long, circled the track in single file, then formed a double lane that turned back inside itself like a movement in a Virginia reel. The circus called this "threading the needle" and it was effective. So was the finish which consisted of the two lanes of horsemen galloping around the track again and passing while going in opposite directions in front of the reserved seats.

The male performers of the circus not employed for the riding acts were expected to fill up the ranks for this number, and I was one of them. What made it a rough assignment was the garland sticks. Each rider had to hold the ends of two sticks in one hand while his other hand held the reins. The sticks were arched and as resilient as a bamboo pole, and they were forever getting away from us and springing back to strike the horse or hit the rider in the face. Also, there was the danger of an inexperienced rider falling off and being trampled by the other horses.

I tumbled the first time around when my horse's pad came off, but I wasn't run down. I caught the horse, mounted bareback and somehow managed to get back into the line.

Unfortunately, this made a hit with Frank Miller who decided then and there that I probably was an experienced equestrian. So when it came time to assign people for their posts in the street parade, he gave me a spirited mount. I was so anxious to make good that I didn't tell him that until that day I never had been on anything faster than a farm plug.

It sure wasn't anything like being on old Charlie and it was still so windy that the flag I carried kept blowing in the horse's face. This scared the horse and the horse scared me. But I managed to make that parade without falling off. Our section wore heavy medieval costumes with leatherette leggings, and we were so near the front of the procession that I never did get to see the whole of it. But one of our balloon vendors who worked the sidewalk uptown told me it was a beautiful sight.

We marched back to the show grounds, turned in our parade wardrobe, had lunch in the cookhouse and dressed for the Garland Entry. When that was over, the riders who also were clowns had only five minutes for getting out of their costumes, changing to clown suits and putting on their makeup for the first clown number. We always made it, but it was always a close call. Bill Langer and I finally decided to stop griping and make a game out of it instead. After that, we raced every day to see who could be ready first and we kept the score on the inside lids of our trunks.

I clowned in whiteface, not the tramp makeup I used later. Zinc oxide and lard I put on my face first, then used a stick of grease paint to outline the eyes and exaggerate the nose and mouth. A neat white costume one of the wardrobe women had made for me quickly, a white wig, and oversize comic shoes completed the get-up. One large tent covered the show's performing or "ring" horses in the center, and was curtained off in end sections to make dressing quarters for the men and women performers. It was commonly called the padroom rather than a dressing tent. The double line of trunks and portable costume racks, collapsible chairs and water buckets belonging to the clowns is always called "clown alley." We had about a dozen clowns in the Howe's Great London show.

In the five minutes between the finish of the Garland Entry and the first clown "breakout," trained ponies worked in the three rings. We could tell when our time was running out because we'd keep one ear turned to the band. The band always plays the same number for the acts and it isn't long before even a person who is tone-deaf gets so he can tell without looking just what is going on in the big top. Circuses all use this system to this day and never have a call-boy as theatres do.

By the time the band played the G-chord for the end of the pony drill, the clowns were at the circus back door or performers' entrance. The equestrian director's whistle blew one short blast, the band changed tempo, and we poured onto the hippodrome track to distribute ourselves so that something would be going on in front of each section of seats. For my first number, I had a large red heart sewed onto the back of my costume with a piece of balsam wood concealed underneath it. Another clown chased me with a hatchet and finally stuck it through the heart. I had to keep replacing the heart because of the holes the hatchet made in it, but I never forgot to wear the wood cushion.

Most clowns don't double in any other act once they have their comic makeup on, and even if they change costumes for their dozen or more appearances in the course of the performance, they wear the same makeup throughout. But because I did a trapeze act, I had to get my makeup off in a hurry and change to my trapeze costume—the same red outfit I had worn in the dog and pony show with the carnival.

I hadn't had any time to rehearse for the circus opening

and the trapeze wasn't rigged properly. I had a hell of a time even getting into the swing, and I made such a mess of the act that when it was over, Frank Miller called me aside and said: "Emmett, it will be easier for you to just clown; we'll forget about the trapeze." That was all right with me, because I didn't get any reduction in salary and I could see that changing back and forth from clown makeup and trapeze costume was going to just about run me ragged. I didn't do any aerial work during the whole tour, but I envied and studied the skillful work done by such performers as Arthur Burson, for I figured I would go back to a trapeze eventually.

Arthur Burson was a middle-aged man then and a good clown. Tall and slender, he had a pleasant and plain face that was all right for makeup and he had the temperament of a true trouper. Rain or shine, hot or cold, easy or rough, he did his work and seldom complained. There wasn't any of the professional jealousy in him that sometimes shows up in actors; he never was too busy or self-important to advise and help the "First-of-May's" and other inexperienced fellows like me. He was my friend then and he still is, for Arthur Burson's trunk is in the "alley" of the "Big One" where he has refreshed my memory on many an incident in this book.

A circus is a place where almost anything can happen and on my first tour just about everything did. The show got into a windstorm in Hastings, Nebraska, and everything blew down except the big top. The boss canvasman stands outside, looking at the sky when a storm is expected, and he has to move fast when it hits. If he thinks the wind is coming ahead of the rain, he orders the guy-out gang to tighten the ropes; if the rain comes first, they slack off because wet circus canvas can get so drum-tight it may tear or even pull up some of the stakes.

This time, the wind came first, and the cookhouse was the first to go. They were trying to get it on the ground, but

59

the storm caught them, and canvas went flying through the air like a wild flag. The side show went next and then the padroom. Fortunately, all this happened between the matinee and the evening performance so there weren't any spectators in the tents.

In a bad blow, the wind gets under the main tent and it begins to billow and strain at its guylines. The quarter poles that are slanted at intervals in front of the seats leave the ground and start swinging free. There is danger of people being batted around by them, so circus prop men and ushers, and anyone else who is handy, wrap arms and legs around them and ride. They try to hold them on the ground with their weight, but often it doesn't do any good. A really tough windstorm may even lift the center poles off the ground a foot or more. A careful boss canvasman will see that there is a stake driven into the ground at every quarter pole in the big top and the pole fastened to it with a loop of rope. Numerous stakes anchor the center poles.

On the day of the storm in Hastings, I got under a wagon and was fairly safe from flying debris and the poles, still attached to the littler tents, that went swinging through the air. But the rain came so fast and hard that I was soon crouching in a pool. Everything and everybody was soaked, and water ran ankle-deep all over the lot as we got busy and rigged clotheslines. Nothing really dried out, but we got the dressing tent up again and elevated our trunks on stakes laid flat while a regular river ran underneath. That night we spread a lot of straw and gave a performance to a few brave customers who were so circus-minded they didn't object to a little wading.

That was my first blow-down, but it didn't cool my ardor for outdoor trouping, nor did the day in Devil's Lake, North Dakota, when the mosquitoes were so bad they broke up the

60

circus parade. Some of the horses threw their riders and rolled in the street to get rid of the stinging swarm.

Before my first circus tour was ended, I was out of the mounted section of the parade and riding on top of the clown bandwagon where I did my best with an old bass horn. It was mostly faking, but eventually I improved because we played the same piece over and over along the line-of-march. Once when we were rolling along a pretty tree-lined street, we saw that a low limb would rake us all off the wagon if we drove under it. Somebody yelled to the driver, but he went right on. We got down on our bellies, but there was very little room and a clown named Tracy Andrews almost hung himself on the limb. He was hopping mad and then and there made a loud speech saying, "I'll never go out with a circus again as long as I live!" But the following spring, Tracy was the first one back.

One morning at daylight the circus train stopped with a jolt that tumbled some of the people out of their bunks. We knew it must be a wreck, so we got off the train and walked up ahead where the stock cars and the flats were. Three flats had derailed, and the wagons had tipped over, but they weren't cages and no animals escaped. One wagon had carried the cookhouse stores and there was so much flour spilled that it looked as if a snowstorm had hit the show. We were there all day while derricks put us back onto the tracks, and of course we lost the town where we had been booked. We simply jumped over it and went on to the next in order to keep our advertised schedule.

I have always had a great fear of train wrecks which I share with a good many outdoor showmen who recall the Hagenbeck-Wallace disaster in the spring of 1918, when the engine of an empty troop train plowed through the sleeping cars of the circus train near Hammond, Indiana, and killed

61

sixty-eight people. Portello, the circus doctor, lived for more than a quarter of a century after the fateful event, claiming that he lived on borrowed time because that night he had given his berth to someone else who died in the crash.

Fifty-six were buried in Showman's Rest, at Woodlawn Cemetery, Chicago, and forty-six of these were unidentified. The Showman's League was only five years old at the time, but its members were determined that no circus or carnival man should go to a potter's field. Today more than six hundred show people rest in this beautiful place, many by choice, and stone elephants silently guard the graves. The first president of the Showman's League of America was Colonel William F. "Buffalo Bill" Cody.

No animals were killed or injured in the Hagenbeck-Wallace wreck, but the show lost so many key personnel that it was hard put to reform its ranks and carry on. That was a war year and help was short, but somehow the show completed its tour. At the wreck of the Walter L. Main Circus train on a sharp curve near Tyrone, Pennsylvania, in 1910, wild animals escaped and ran in all directions. One panther that never was captured lived on for years in the mountains and carried off plenty of livestock from nearby farms.

In the old "mud-show" days before circuses started traveling by rail, the shows would advertise that they would play a town "on or about" such and such a date. They never knew how long it would take them to pull the heavy equipment through the muddy roads or ford through creeks and rivers where the bridges weren't strong enough to support the wagons. One of the old Barnum records says that fourteen horses were needed to pull a hippopotamus cage overland in those days, and one of the old stories handed down claims that after a particularly rugged night the driver of the first wagon to sight the show's destination would shout "China!," meaning that the show had plowed its way clear through the earth.

Howe's Great London outfit was a "grift" show, which is the name given to a circus that carries gamblers to lure suckers into games in which they try to discover which shell the pea is under, or where the ace is when a clever manipulator shows three playing cards and keeps moving them around so that the sucker can see the faces before the manipulator arranges them face-down.

This occasionally made for plenty of trouble. Even though the show's "patch" or "fixer," as the legal adjuster was nicknamed, had invariably slipped some money to the chief of police so that these grifters could operate in violation of the law, the fellow who had been fleeced might round up his friends and start a battle on the lot or make trouble at the trains when the show was loading.

Sometimes there would be a notice posted in the dressing room, ordering the troupe to go directly to the cars after the night performance and not go uptown. This was the tip-off that there was trouble and that any circus man caught away from his own crowd ran a good chance of being beaten up. More than one grift show rolled out of town with its people lying flat on the floors of the sleeping cars while rifle shots and bursts from shotguns blasted the windows.

In one town where we had been warned to go straight to the cars, Lloyd Center and I broke the rule to keep a date with some town girls. They had given us the eye during the afternoon performance and we had met them later and arranged to see them at the edge of the lot that night.

Of course, quite a few of the show people saw us sneak through a hole in the fence when we were supposed to be going the other direction and they kidded us, but nobody squealed to the management. The girls were there all right and we asked if we could walk them home. We didn't want to risk taking them uptown to an ice-cream parlor. As we went farther and farther from the show train, I began to be worried. Most of the townspeople were in bed and the streets were quiet, but a block away under a street lamp there was a crowd of fellows with clubs. One of them yelled: "I saw them leave the show grounds and I think they came this way."

That was enough for me. I had started to take down the address of my date so I could write to her, but I never finished. The gallant circus men excused themselves and took off.

The town gang had spotted us by then and ran after us. Lloyd and I ducked through an alley, ran over gardens and finally got lost. It took us a long time to find the show train because we were afraid to ask directions and when we did spot the train, it was pulling out. We were winded, but turned on a final burst of speed and just caught the last car.

One night there was a fight on the midway and one of the men who appeared in our Wild West Concert, or after-show, was hit over the head with a whiskey bottle. He staggered back to the dressing tent and we started picking glass out of his scalp. "I don't care," he said cheerfully. "I was bareheaded. They didn't hurt my forty-dollar Stetson!"

I did a little cartooning just for fun and so I wouldn't get out of practice during that tour, and one day Murphy asked me to draw a caricature of our assistant manager, Whitey Azel. I forget what situation I was to put him in, but apparently it all went back to something that I didn't know about and I was in hot water without knowing why.

When I returned from parade and was climbing down off the clown bandwagon with my battered old horn, Dan Odum called me over. "Did you draw that cartoon?"

I said that I had done it and that they had paid me fifty cents for doing it and reimbursed me for paper and other materials. "Well, you're fired," Odum said. "I'll have no trouble started around here because of pictures that make the executives sore. Go pack up and get off the lot."

He asked me who put me up to doing it, but I refused to

64

My father.

My mother, my sister,
and I (aged three).

At eighteen I left the farm.

My debut as a trapeze performer, 1922.

(Theatrical Studio, Chicago)

"The Aerial Kellys."
My first wife, Eva, and I.

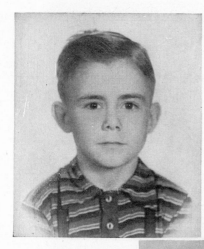

Thomas Patrick Kelly.

MY
TWO SONS

Emmett Leo Kelly, Jr.

THE
EVOLUTION
OF
WILLIE

(*Upper left*) Willie as I first conceived him, 1922. (*Upper right*) A variation. (*Lower left*) A start in the mournful direction. (*Lower right*) Willie at the age of ten.

Advertising the Hagenbeck-Wallace Circus.

(*Don Smith*, *Detroit*)

A new costume
and a new prop
— an explosive
spittoon.

The famous boondoggling act of 1936 (Cole Bros.-Clyde
Beatty Circus).

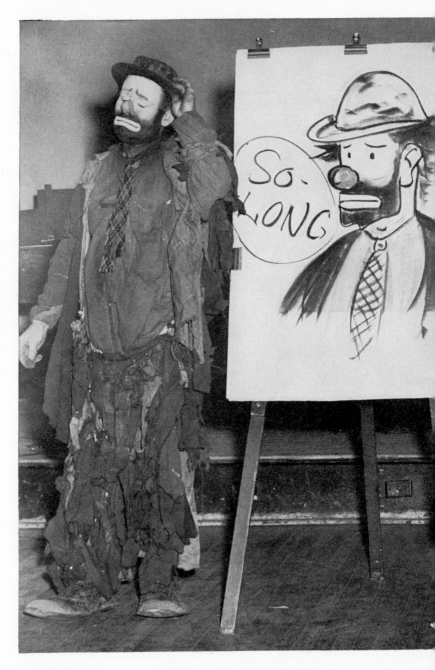

My cartoonist act—finale.

My first Hollywood part—as Ed Deets, a circus clown, I confess to
three murders in Universal-International's *The Fat Man*.

Making up for the role

(Universal Pictures Company, Inc.)

d Deets in *The Fat Man*.

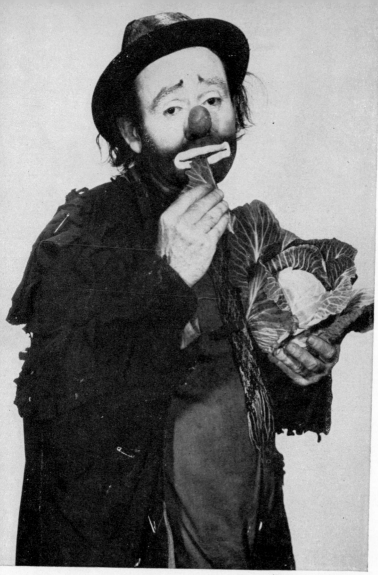

In Cecil B. DeMille's Academy Award winning *The Greatest
Show On Earth* I played myself—or, rather, Willie.

With James Stewart as a brother clown
in *The Greatest Show On Earth.*

Clowning in Scotland with the Mills Circus.

Back home again, with a new routine.

Clown Alley.

tell him. I went back to the padroom, dejected, and started to put my things in the trunk. Kenneth Waite asked me what I was up to. "I'm fired," I told him, "over that cartoon."

"They can't do that to you, Emmett," he said. "You didn't know anything about the motives in the thing; you just drew what they told you. I'll go to the boss myself."

Whatever he told the manager must have cooled him off, because Odum sent for me. "Okay, Kelly," he said now. "I understand that you were the innocent party in the scheme. And you don't have to tell me who started it. I know. And you aren't fired."

Howe's Great London played all over the map. We showed all the way down into Florida as far as Fort Myers, and at Tampa we had to give three performances to get the crowd in. In late autumn we closed in Alabama, where the band played "Auld Lang Syne" and everybody said goodbye. The office wagon paid off at the railroad loading runs. All circuses had a policy known as the hold-back. They retained one week's pay throughout the season and you got it at the end of the tour if you were there. If you left the show before it closed, you lost the hold-back. This was not a bad policy, for it was an inducement to people to remain for the whole season and it also gave every employee some money in the closing town so nobody would be stranded there broke.

The troupe was welcome to ride the train back to winter quarters, but there were a good many performers who went in other directions to fill vaudeville dates and other off-season employment. Most of the show's labor rode the train home, although only a few of them were retained at quarters to re-build the circus for the next tour and to care for the animals.

On the home run, there was a continuous crap game, but I stayed out of it. From my weekly salary of twenty-five bucks, I had managed to save only eighty-five dollars and I was in the market for winter work. Dan Odum had told me that he was going to manage John Robinson's Circus the next year and that I could go to work for that larger show the following spring, but I had a hard time between circus jobs.

I had made friends with a tall, muscular, good-looking fellow and his pint-size red-headed wife—George and Mae Clark—who did a double-trapeze act, and they let me live with them in a one-room arrangement. The Clarks slept in the only bed and I slept on the sofa. They were broke, too, and we struggled through the winter by posing as amateurs and entering contests in theatres. We always grabbed off first and second place and pooled our winnings. We cooked in the room and just barely got by. When I was hungry and feeling blue, I'd remember that Mr. Whitcomb had predicted this kind of thing when I left the Adv. Film Company. But I never was discouraged enough to consider for one minute the possibility of giving up the circus.

Down the hall from our cold-water flat there was a pretty girl who was badly crippled. We used to have her in to play checkers and she was cheerful company. When I'd get to feeling sorry for myself, I'd think about this girl who never complained about her handicap and I'd be ashamed.

I got some work for a while with a commercial movie place where I was paid seventy-five cents a card for piecework lettering. This didn't last long, but they let the Clarks and me rig our equipment in the basement and practice.

I was too proud to tell my folks what a thin time I was having, but from the lettering job I saved enough money to go home for Christmas and take some simple presents.

Then we got a break. We were signed on at the St. Louis Police Circus, which was a collection of acts presented for two weeks in a big building, circus-style, with the profits going to police charities.

At the very first performance, I fell from my swing and dropped thirty feet. I remember hearing someone in the audience scream, and then I blacked out. The fall only stunned me because the dirt on the arena floor wasn't packed down hard yet and the new sawdust was thick. I shook some sense back into my spinning head and climbed back up. By this time, everybody in the place was watching me and when I finished even the circus people joined in applause that rocked the building.

I never fell again. Circus performing is loaded with danger, but seldom is there a serious accident. Circus doctors and first-aid people get most of their patients from the labor personnel who can get hurt in a dozen different ways every day as they handle heavy equipment at top speed. By the time an aerialist is skilled enough to work for an important circus, he has reduced his hazards to a minimum. Only flying-trapeze or casting acts work over nets. They must have a net beneath them because the leapers fly free through space from the swinging bar to the hands of the catcher. This is split-second, precision work and they do fall from time to time. Even then they can get hurt, for the net is tight and hitting it out of control can break an arm, a leg or a neck.

My pleasure at being recognized around the Police Circus as a real trouper who completed his act after a fall was diluted by a sudden problem that almost cost me my summer job. I had expected to join the John Robinson show the Monday after the final Saturday of the Police Circus, but I read in the *Billboard* that John Robinson's Circus would open in its winter quarters town, Peru, Indiana, on Friday. I sent a wire and asked if I could join a few days late and quickly got an answer reading, "Sorry but cannot place you after opening."

I went to David Murphy, boss of the Police show, who turned out to be a swell guy. He could have held me to my contract and made me finish out the week, but instead he let me go. He even paid me for the full engagement, but I knew this was a mistake and went to him about it. "By golly, Em-

83

mett," he said, "you are an honest man. A lot of guys wouldn't do that. You can always work for me again."

Rich farmland between the Wabash and the Missisinewa rivers three miles east of Peru was the winter home of John Robinson's Circus. It had been the old stamping ground for Ben Wallace before Jerry Mugivan, Bert Bowers and Ed Ballard bought his show and set up the American Circus Corporation. Their biggest circus was Sells-Floto, formerly owned by Bonfils and Tammen of the *Denver Post,* and they operated the Robinson show and Hagenbeck-Wallace, too. This was a big outfit with a lot of holdings including the Wabash Valley Bank and Trust Company in Peru, and their circuses were the main competition for the larger Ringling Brothers and Barnum & Bailey show.

I made that date with no time to spare. John Robinson's tents were in the air with all flags flying and the parade was lined up in the street when I hurried back to the dressing tent to report to a well-built, medium-height, distinguished-looking man in riding breeches and highly polished boots. He was Fred Leggett, the equestrian director and he was busier than a bear in a bee hive. "Where the hell have you been?" was his greeting. "The parade is ready and you are supposed to ride a wagon."

I got into a costume in a rush and climbed aboard while the wagon was moving. There was no time to rig my trapeze in the opening town, so I didn't go up until we were in Marion, Indiana, next day.

I was in trouble right away. Not because of the act—it went very well—but right afterward Fred Leggett drew me aside and said: "Don't wear red tights. Mr. Mugivan doesn't like red except on circus wagons. Get pink, blue—anything but red, and get yourself a set of whites."

Of course I had to send to Chicago for them and in the meantime I had nothing to wear but red. I tightened up every time I saw Mugivan in the tent during my act. When payday came, I lined up at the office wagon with the rest of the performers, but they didn't call my name. The treasurer fumbled through a pile of envelopes when I asked for mine and said, "I have nothing for you."

"Well, I am working under contract and I have been here all week," I said.

Mugivan was in the wagon, a pile of contracts in his hand. That big circus office wagon didn't seem big enough for Jerry Mugivan. He managed to almost fill it although he was not fat—just tall and impressive to look at. It was his personality, I guess, that took up so much space. He had a big, handsome head, still blond except for just a shade of white at the temples. His features were Irish and in his perfectly manicured hand he held an expensive cigar.

The smoke drifted through the window as Mugivan went slowly through the contracts. Finally he turned to his treasurer. "Yes, I seem to have one here for Kelly. He gets twenty-five." Then he looked at me and smiled a little, but only with his eyes, and said nothing. I figured he probably had his mind on those blasted red tights.

Soon, however, I had a baby-blue "wardrobe" and white tights, too. The trapeze singles always carried two or more sets and wore what they pleased, but the members of the flying-return acts all wore the same color at each appearance. The head of the act, which had three or more persons in it, would look up his partners well in advance of the turn and yell, "White today," or "Blue today" or whatever it was he had decided on.

Eddie Ward was in charge of our flying acts and was the best-known name in that phase of the business. This tall, handsome Hoosier with big shoulders and slim legs and the split-second timing of a precision instrument in his brain, trained dozens of youngsters in his winter quarters barn at

85

Bloomington, Illinois, and some of them became great. Several even took his last name for professional use.

One day, we showed on a lake-front lot that had a good deal of soft, deep sand where the dressing top was pitched. Eddie and some other comedians who didn't mind working hard to put over a good joke went out to the lot early. They dug holes and buried half the trunks, and we had a hell of a time digging them up. Another time, somebody put cactus dust in the tights worn by our Arab tumblers. It drove them half crazy. Never before had they tumbled so wildly nor finished their act so fast. They came back to the dressing tent fighting mad, but everybody looked innocent and had no explanation for them—only sympathy. A fellow named Fred Young on that show was a great hand to light matches stuck into the shoes of a sleeping performer and give him a "hot-foot." It was a sure bath with a bucket of water in the face if any of us dared to fall asleep on the ground between shows. There was more comedy in the circus backyard that tour than the clowns could manage to give the customers in the big top.

The circus wound its way through the Southwest toward Dixie, and in Galveston, Texas, half the show was sick with fever from mosquito bites. Of course we put the show on anyhow since there's nothing in a circus contract about laying off when you don't feel up to scratch. If you missed a performance. you'd be docked one-twelfth of a week's pay. Of course the management didn't expect anyone to perform if he was very sick, but it took a mighty bad pain to keep a real trouper from working.

When we closed that season in Tennessee, I had saved a couple of hundred dollars. I rode the show train as far as Indianapolis and got a job in a glove factory without wasting any time. I remembered vividly the previous winter lay-offs in St. Louis and what a rough time it had been, and I wanted no more unemployment or, as we say in show business, the unfortunate condition of being "at liberty."

Meanwhile my folks had sold their place in Texas County and were ready to go and live with my brother-in-law on a farm near Mulberry Grove, Illinois. My dad had a stroke while shucking corn; I was notified by telegram, and I hurried home. I'll never forget my dad's face when I put my arms around him.

The moving now was quite a problem because of the condition of my father, but we packed everything and got a cot and loaded Dad into a baggage car because we couldn't get him into a coach. I remember that I had to go and see the railroad officials and get a clearance by stating that my father had no contagious disease. I rode with him in the baggage car. At St. Louis I explained to a passenger agent that I wanted to get on a fast train—one that never stopped at the little town of Mulberry Grove. He agreed to stop the train there and issued an order. It was the first time that flier ever had stopped there and the whole town turned out to see what was going on.

My folks settled on a farm of only about seventy acres there and while Father managed to sit up in a wheel chair after a while, he never recovered and died the next year. I was traveling with the circus in eastern Canada and did not find out about it until the funeral service was over.

When I had helped to settle my folks on the new farm, I hurried back to Indianapolis, quit my job at the glove factory and high-tailed it for St. Louis, where I managed to squeeze in another engagement with the Police Circus before returning to John Robinson's Circus for the spring opening.

One day that season, a short, wiry, curly-haired young fellow from Bainbridge, Ohio, walked onto the lot and asked for a job as a cage boy. He was crazy about wild animals, especially the big cats. I got to know him soon after he went to work and we spent a lot of time palling around together. The job of a cage boy drew low pay and it was hard work. Just keeping the dens clean is a problem and it must be done twice a day because otherwise the cat animals get headaches from the high percentage of ammonia in the urine. If they are performers, this adds to the trainer's hazard. The new cage boy tied into that job as if he really meant it, and he must have because in less than ten years his name was up in lights in front of Madison Square Garden for the Ringling Brothers and Barnum & Bailey spring engagement and he was giving the big town goose pimples every time he stepped into the steel arena with forty jungle-bred lions and tigers. But the day he joined John Robinson's Circus, he was broke and hungry and the timekeeper had no reason to be impressed when he looked at the name scribbled on the payroll and saw that it was Clyde Beatty.

Eva and Mitzie Moore did a sister act in double trapeze with the show that season of 1923, and I fell in love with Eva. She was tiny and slim although muscular in the right places without bulging. She had curly blond hair with a nice sheen to it. She had talent and courage and a liking for me. We sat on wardrobe trunks in the circus backyard while the same old moon looked down at us in many different towns. We'd pretend that the band was serenading just us instead of all the customers in the big top when it played a romantic number like "The Same Silvery Moon" or "A Pretty Girl Is Like a Melody."

The problem was Old Man Moore, who didn't want his kids to get married and maybe leave the show and break up the act. The circus manager warned me several times that Eva's father didn't want us to go together. "You've got to cut out running around with this girl," he said. "I'm sick and tired of hearing her old man crabbing about it." Moore was a cocky

88

little rooster with plenty of savvy about aerial work and never afraid to speak his mind.

One day when the circus was playing in Niagara Falls, we slipped off between shows and went across to the Canadian side where a carnival was playing. While we were riding on the Ferris wheel, I proposed. Eva was afraid that if we got married we would both be fired—or at least I would be. I remember saying "The hell with that; we'll get married anyhow. I don't think they'll run us off the show."

Well, the upshot of it was that we found we couldn't get married in Canada and so we put it off until the show was in Charlottesville, Virginia, on the twenty-first of July. We went downtown to the courthouse in the morning to buy a license and after the matinee we sneaked off to the home of a preacher and were married in his front parlor. I didn't like the dress my wife had on because it didn't fit very well and I thought it was too fancy. So the first thing I bought her was a new dress.

Back on the lot, Eva showed the girls her ring and there was a lot of excitement in the dressing tent. I was feeling pretty proud and happy until the manager came to me and said, "Come into the office wagon, I want to talk to you."

"Well, I guess I'm fired," I said by way of starting the conversation.

"Why are you fired?" Dan Odum asked.

"Because I married Eva Moore an hour ago."

Odum blew smoke from his cigar and looked off into space. "I wish you had told me ahead of time. I might have bought you a baby buggy or something."

"Well, are we fired or do we stay?" I asked.

"You stay on," the boss answered, "but you've got to go and face the girl's old man."

I went to my new father-in-law and told him, "We just got married, Mr. Moore. How do I stand with you now?"

89

I thought he took it pretty well. "Nothing I can do about it now but make the best of it," was his answer.

Eva and I were given a lower berth on the circus train, and, believe me, getting married was about the only way a man could get one. That's how tight the space was. In less than two weeks, when the wife of a trapeze performer named Levan Rotavia left the show because she was going to have a baby, Dan Odum sent for me to ask if I would like to have him move Mitzie Moore into the Rotavia double-trapeze act and team up with Eva.

A circus big top is a busy place between the afternoon and the evening performance because performers use it for practicing new tricks and perfecting old ones. Eva and I re-hearsed hard with the help of her dad who had trained all his kids—eight of them.

The Moore girls, besides Eva, were Grace, Mitzie, Gladys and Bertha. There were two boys, also—Dinky and Robert. Those kids, like most circus families, were versatile. They had learned to do just about everything, including a very good roller-skating act.

My bride and I worked well in double trapeze, which is simply a swing wide enough for two, and the act went well until one day when we were doing hand and foot exchanges she got away from me and fell twenty-seven feet. Luckily the ground was sandy, but she broke her wrist. I went back to single trapeze, and Eva was shifted to the job of taking tickets with one hand in one of the grandstand sections. The other hand was in a sling. Eva and I made fifty bucks a week between us and the management didn't reduce her salary when she switched to the new job.

That winter we did light housekeeping in Indianapolis. Eva's wrist healed and she worked on our costumes while I went back to work at the glove factory. A nice guy named McNeil, who was superintendent of the State Fair grounds, let several of us circus families hang our rigging and practice in the coliseum, so we were in shape when we got a call to work the St. Louis Police Circus once more.

We joined the Robinson show again and that tour found me busy with my drawing board in my spare time. I had made a sketch for a letterhead for Eva and me, showing three feature tricks performed by "The Aerial Kellys," and now I drew cartoons of the things that happened around the show. One was a composite of the principal performers and I was very proud when the show's press agent, Doc Stewart, got it into print in a Canadian newspaper.

Eva and I worked double trapeze as before and we got a raise in salary because I doubled as a whiteface clown. This gave me a mighty busy timetable, but we were going to have a baby and I wanted to save every cent we could. Eva rode a horse in the street parade and I played a bass drum on the clown bandwagon.

I was fooling around with the idea of doing in the flesh the little sad-faced hobo clown who had been born on my drawing board back in Kansas City at the Adv. Film Company, but when I tried it out in the show, the boss clown, Kenneth Waite, didn't like it. He was a "neat" clown type and said the tramp impersonation looked dirty.

I was so offended that I got my Irish up and went to the manager. "I can't go over Waite's head in a case like this," he told me. "He's the boss of the clown department and you will have to do as he says if you want to stay with the circus."

I was mad enough to quit on the spot, but remembering a father's responsibilities cooled me considerably. I went back to clowning in whiteface, but "Willie," which was the name I gave in my mind to my tramp character, kept wandering around in there and nudging me so I wouldn't forget him entirely.

Our boy was born in Dyersburg, Tennessee, on Novem-

ber 24, the closing day of the circus tour. Eva had worked in
the trapeze act until two months before the baby was due, and
had been shifted to a ticket-taking job during that period. If
Emmett, Jr. had waited two or three more days, he would have
been safe at home in Indiana, but he was bound to be born on
the circus.

It was a cold, rainy day, and when I came down out of
the rigging, one of the circus women told me that my wife
would have to start for the hospital right away. I changed so
fast I forgot to put my socks on, and we raced for the hospital
where the baby arrived about three hours later. He was small,
but well-developed and looked absolutely perfect to his old
man. He had big ears and a pug nose and so much hair that
he looked as though he was wearing burnsides—as I was in
those days when *The Sheik* was a movie and a popular song
and hot-shots of the day copied Rudolph Valentino.

The show train was leaving next day, but some of the
circus women managed to squeeze in a fast trip to the hospital
with a pile of neatly wrapped presents for Eva and the baby.

My wife and I had got into a number of arguments about
money during that circus tour and I suppose I did pinch the
pennies a bit. But from sad experience I knew how long a
winter can be for circus people when there is no work. Anyhow, our son wasn't born broke. His pappy had saved eight
hundred dollars and converted it proudly into traveler's checks
of twenty-dollar denominations. In two weeks, when Eva and
our boy were ready to leave, we set off for the farm near Mulberry Grove. We stayed there with my mother and my
sister Sylvia and her husband until after Christmas when we
went back to Indianapolis. I got my old job back in the glove
company's shipping room and rented a place for my family
a block away.

As springtime approached, we went back to practicing in
the State Fair coliseum. There was some heat in the building,

so we were able to take the boy along and park him in his little crib where he slept while his parents high overhead took risks that could have made him an orphan.

Since there was no chance to go back to the Robinson Circus that spring, because they would not carry people with small children, I booked our double "trap" act with a show called Rogers and Harris for one hundred and fifty dollars a week. This was a nice boost and the only drawback was that the show went bust after only fifteen weeks, owing us almost nine hundred in back pay. We had a blow-down, too, in Memphis. Everything went but the little dressing tent that Eva, the baby, and I had to ourselves. I had it guyed out tight and it held.

We had bought a Ford roadster and a camping outfit for that trip, so we could set up by ourselves at some convenient spot on the show grounds where we could keep an eye on the boy and live in some privacy. Now, as we headed for home, we knew that late August is no time to be finishing a circus tour. We had to find employment, so I scratched around the booking agencies and got us a couple of appearances at fairs. The money was pretty good, but we didn't work as regularly as we did under circus management. We dropped anchor at the farm near Mulberry Grove and went back and forth in our car to whatever dates the booking office lined up for us.

The rest of the time our rigging was hung in the yard and it was that summer I taught myself to hang by my teeth. This is called an iron-jaw act and a lot of people think it is easy. It appears that the thing the performer puts into his mouth locks in there so he can't fall. Actually the gadget or "grip" is merely a piece of hard rubber with the user's teeth impressions in it and shaped so that he can get his mouth around it.

I made my grip from two rubber heels, had a harness maker fix me a strapping with a ring in it, and got a swivel from a hardware store. My object was to hang upside down in the trapeze swing, and with my teeth hold a strap which had a pole hanging from it. Eva was to swing and spin and do simple tricks on this vertical pole. She weighed a hundred pounds and I weighed about a hundred and fifty, so I knew that if I could make my jaws support my weight, I could handle Eva without too much trouble. For a good many rehearsals I had to hang mostly from my hands. Little by little, my jaws got strong enough to take the weight.

Eva and I worked well together. We always did a fast act with plenty of snap in it, and the addition of the iron-jaw routine made it possible for me to ask for more money when we booked the act.

When autumn came around, we drove South to try to pick up some work with the Southern fairs, but had no luck at all. They had signed up their grandstand attractions a long time in advance of the exhibitions. I was getting discouraged when I drove through a little town in Tennessee and saw a poster advertising the Mighty Haag show. This was the first circus I had seen, as a seventeen-year-old kid. A man in a blacksmith shop told me which direction the show trucks had gone, and we drove on to where I saw one of the show trucks had broken down and had been left behind in a garage. The mechanic told me where he thought the circus had gone, but when we reached that town we found we were still one day behind it. The roads got worse and worse, but at last we saw the tents on the edge of a very small town. I drove onto the lot and there, luckily enough, ran into a fellow I knew named Abe Johnson.

A family of aerialists had just left the show and so we were in luck. The pay was only twenty-five dollars a week, but it was better than loafing, and the cookhouse wasn't bad. It was a way to put in the rest of the circus season and maybe save a bit against the winter months. The Mighty Haag show looked mighty small and beat-down compared to a big outfit

94

like John Robinson's, still it was a popular outfit in the small towns and villages of the South. The tent was so low, however, that I'd almost touch the ground when I hung upside down in the trapeze, and of course, we could not attempt the iron-jaw routine.

I don't know where they ever found some of the towns we showed in. One of them was nothing but a feed mill, a general store and a church, and I didn't think we'd play to fifty people. However, by nightfall, I could see hundreds of lantern lights bobbing on the mountain paths, and before the show our tent was jammed to capacity. This was rough country with plenty of moonshine and the fighting that goes with it. An odd thing, though, was that the toughs who got loaded and picked fights never bothered the circus people, but always fought each other.

Old man Haag often had to stop the show and make a speech, telling the trouble-makers to settle down or he'd call off the performance, since some of the more festive customers would get to feeling so good they'd whip out a gun and shoot small holes in the top of the tent. Haag paid us off in silver. All salaries and wages were so small that he probably figured it felt like more money if it was hard cash. After each payday, there'd be a rush for the stores so the silver could be changed into paper money. Haag gave the local tradesmen circus passes in exchange for fodder and other feed, and he could stretch a dollar farther than any operator I ever saw. I think he ran that circus for about three hundred dollars a day. Once when we pitched our canvas next to a good-sized turkey farm the birds came over to visit like curious kids. Something frightened them up on the ridge of the main tent where they roosted all night. No one was accused of molesting them next morning when the show was dismantled, but I remember that we had turkey on the table for several days thereafter.

Like most truck shows, Mighty Haag did its traveling in

the early morning, but not before dawn. The show would remain on the lot all night, then move to the next town. It is dangerous to run heavy circus trucks at night and there is also the chance that somebody will take a wrong turn and get lost. The trail is blazed by white chalk marks on telephone poles and trees, and one could cause a rival show unlimited difficulty by changing these chalk marks and sending the trucks off in different directions.

Old man Haag was pretty strict about drinking and he was firmly against smoking. He went to church and liked to talk about religion but we all liked the old guy who looked like an Ozark preacher and dressed the part, too. The band leader had his little boy on the Haag show and gave him the circus owner's name. The kid was learning to play the cornet and I guess you'd have to say he mastered it if you've ever listened to Harry Haag James. When the circus finally closed on the seventeenth of December, there was a ceremony in the tent to present the owner with a trophy cup. This unexpected affair so unnerved the old boy that he dropped the trophy in the mud. He was a good man to work for, and all things considered, we hadn't had too bad a year.

I had forty bucks left over when we got back to Indianapolis and made the final payment on the car before buying Christmas presents and heading for Mulberry Grove. Our boy had grown a lot and my mother was delighted with him. He was a good little fellow and never had been sick enough to need a doctor. The outdoor life seemed to be good for him.

I was forced to borrow a little money from the folks to take my family back to Indianapolis, but it was the first time I ever had to do it and, I am happy to say, the last.

Nobody in show business, especially outdoor show business, is ever really broke. You can be hungry, and I know the feeling. You can be lonely and I know about that, too. You can be scared and I've been—plenty. But there is so much to draw on in the bank of friendship and sympathy and excitement and hope that you just never feel that you are really busted.

I've noticed that not many show people are suicides. They may die broke or sick or unhappy, but they seldom give up hope. They are so used to the "miracles" of this crazy business—the unaccountable ups and downs, the sudden rainbow after the storm—that they just can't quite settle for the idea that the deck is stacked, the wheel fixed, the dice frozen or the whole game rigged against them. Show people are hopeful people, like children looking forward to Christmas or to a birthday cake. Worldly and sophisticated though they are, they seem to have so much simple faith that everything will be okay tomorrow! Even their hope of Heaven is so natural, so childlike in its belief, that I'm sure Saint Peter must have passed a lot of show folks through that "main entrance."

I mortgaged the car for a hundred dollars, paid back the folks on the farm, paid our friend at the State Fair coliseum who had loaned us money earlier, and set out to find work.

The glove company wouldn't take me on again because I had left them every spring, but I finally talked myself into a job with a wholesale grocery company. I first told the boss I wanted it just for the rest of the winter, but he wouldn't hire me that way. "I want men who will stay here and learn the business. We promote them fast in this place," he assured me. Well, if they had promoted me to president inside one week I'd not have given up the circus, but I told him a lie to get the job. "I'm not going back to the circus," I said. "I'll stay on as long as you want me."

They paid me nineteen dollars a week. Our grocery bill didn't run much over five dollars, our rent was five dollars and at twelve cents apiece we managed about one movie a week.

The Police Circus management at St. Louis wrote to me

in care of Eva's family at Peru, Indiana, asking me to state my price for their nine-day engagement. I asked two hundred dollars and got it. So Eva and I started practicing again at the fair grounds, and now it came time to tell the man at the grocery warehouse that I was quitting. He was sore as hell. "I knew it, I *knew* it; you're quitting to go back to the circus! You promised to stay. I swear, I'll never hire another showman as long as I live!"

"Well, I know you've got a right to be mad at me," I told him, "but this is somewhat unusual. You see, I have a chance to make some pretty good money."

I showed him my circus contract and he nearly jumped out of his shoes. "You mean they pay *that* kind of money?"

"They sure as hell do—to a good act," I said as I marched off with what I hoped was an air of offended dignity.

I had a contract to return to the Robinson show again and we had planned to leave our boy with my mother for the touring season. But one day I got a letter from the show's manager that read:

Dear Mr. Kelly,

Upon looking over your contract, we find that you are engaged to do double trapeze and two cloud swings. We are not using double trapeze this year, so would you mind doing a single and doubling in clowning while your wife works the ladder act?

I got really mad at this and wired back that I would not consider it.

I didn't want to go back to clowning unless I could do my tramp character and I knew that the boss clown wouldn't stand for that. Still, no more whiteface clowning for me, so I took a crack at the smaller Gentry Brothers Circus, and told them we would come on with our double-trapeze act for sixty-five a week, the salary I had been promised by the Robinson show. The contract came back all right, but for ten dollars less.

It was too late to fool around any more, so we packed up and went to Fort Knox, where in deserted army buildings the Gentry show had its winter quarters. The show was already in rehearsal and the band was playing in the big top, a patched and ugly-looking spread of canvas if I ever saw one. I called aside an old trouper I had known on another show and said, "Give me the low-down; what about this thing?"

He looked around to make sure nobody could hear us and replied, "You can see it's a gypsy camp. And it looks like we got half the 'lucky boys' (the nickname for grifters) in the business."

I then went to look at the sleeping cars which were cramped and shabby. Then and there, Eva and I decided that no matter what we might have to do on the Robinson show, it would beat this. So we rounded up our baggage and took off, catching the Robinson show a few days after its opening. The manager was understanding about the whole thing and said, "Look, Emmett, you don't belong with that show; you belong here. I'm glad to see you back."

I never had felt so good. I was home again, and I stayed for several years without interruption. John Robinson's Circus isn't on the road any more. It was put away nearly twenty-five years ago, not long after the Ringling organization bought the American Circus Corporation, but people still ask for it—especially in Dixie. The show had great popularity in the South, where it had started traveling on river boats out of Cincinnati before the Civil War. It was the oldest circus in the country in point of continuous operation, and although it was smaller than several of its big-time competitors, it could play day-and-date against even the Barnum show and do business in Dixie.

This story has been told oftener than the one about the farmer's daughter, but I'm going to tell it again because it illustrates the loyalty of the people in the South toward the Robinson outfit. A colored lady with her little boy tugging at her skirts was looking at a poster for the Barnum & Bailey Circus, advertising the coming of the show on the first day of September.

"What do it say?" asked the boy.

His mother read slowly and replied, "It say that de Barnum an' Bailey Circus am de 'greatest show on earth' 'cept one, an' dat am Massa John Robinson's Circus!"

In the spring of 1928, the Robinson show tried to open in West Baden, Indiana, where it had wintered that year. The lot was on low ground and spring rains had turned the place into a swamp where the water ran four feet deep. They had to lower the big top and float it off on poles, and they left the bleachers and grandstand to be sent for several days later— after the water had gone down. Meanwhile, the show had cancelled several stands and moved on to Louisville for a fresh start.

This was the beginning of an exciting but disastrous tour. The show had twenty-one straight days of rain in Canada. Day after day we wore damp clothing. Night after night the tents, their weight tripled by the water they had absorbed, were loaded soaking wet. We lost two giraffes that tour, each of which had cost ten thousand dollars.

In Bangor, Maine, one of Mabel Stark's tigers nearly tore her to pieces in full view of the crowd. Mabel was the first woman ever to break, train and present tigers, and she worked alone. Nobody went into the big cage with her except fourteen Bengal and Sumatran beauties. She weighed less than a hundred pounds, but she even handled all her heavy props alone. She carried no revolver, loaded with blanks, but worked with only a whip and a chair. It was a beautiful thing to see, and although not a young woman then, Mabel's blond hair, trim costume and lithe bearing gave the act a lot of class.

She had been clawed up before, but she still loved her tigers. Always, after an accident, she would say it was her fault; to hear her tell it, the murderous bundles of striped fury never were to blame.

In a wild-animal act, the chair is useful because it not only is bulk protection when held between the trainer and a rushing cat, but the four separate legs seem to confuse the mind of the animal and slow the attack. Trainers try to keep on their little pedestals all the big cats except the one that is doing a trick. When they are seated, the animals aren't in a good position to attack. It's when they roam free on the floor of the cage that they're most dangerous. And, of course, if a trainer trips and falls, he's in a very vulnerable position.

The cat that got Mabel that night was one of her favorites. She had raised it from a cub in the kitchen of her home in California. These circus-born kittens nearly always grow up to be trouble-makers because they have been petted when babies and have lost their fear of people. The first rule to remember in that end of the circus business is that there is no such thing as a tamed wild animal. You can train them, but nobody can ever be sure that they're *tamed*.

There are men with loaded rifles on the outside of the steel arenas during the presentation of such acts, but the cats move so fast that the riflemen are likely to shoot the trainer instead of the cat. Once when a lion and a tiger got into a fight in Clyde Beatty's big cage during the filming of a movie in Hollywood, it took a firehose to break it up.

Usually somebody has to go into the arena and get the trainer out when he has been attacked by a tiger or a lion or some other wild animal. This night, Bobby Thornton, the equestrian director, and Terrell Jacobs, who had the lion act, went in and drove off the cat that took on Mabel.

101

I had just left the padroom and was on my way to the big top when they carried her out, in an armlock, blood streaming down her legs. Somebody was yelling for a stretcher and I knew there wasn't any, so I ran and got a folding army cot and we put her on that.

At the hospital, she was still conscious and able to direct the doctors, knowing from experience how quickly infection sets in from the teeth and claw wounds of the big meat-eaters. She had them pour raw carbolic acid directly into the wounds.

The show went on without her, of course, and it was touch-and-go for the game little woman for some weeks. Still she was back on the show by the time we were in Columbus, Ohio, and she didn't come back just to visit. She came back to work the cats.

Swathed in bandages and walking with a cane, she started rehearsing them back into the routine singly and in pairs until she had the cage full and the act in shape to present before many days had passed. Mabel's body is a network of scars, or, in her own words, medals, and she's still working animals in a zoo in California. She's handled tigers, lions, bears, leopards and jaguars, but the tigers remain her first love.

It was in Oil City, Pennsylvania, that a lion got loose and took off across the backyard without the crowd in the big top knowing anything was wrong. I was testing my rigging and was about ready to do my act when another performer whispered to me what was going on out back. "If he comes in here, you'll see me on top of this rigging," I replied, and over the music of the band he yelled in my ear, "Just make room for me!"

When I had finished my turn, I went into the back yard and learned that the lion was some distance away, underneath a clump of trees. There was an embankment over a little creek at the end of the show grounds, and when I looked over there I saw as pretty a sight as I ever hope to see. There stood the

102

big cat, on the rise of ground, peering across the water while the wind kept blowing his mane. It looked like a painting of a scene on the African veldt.

They finally rounded him up with canvas sidewall and shifted him into his cage in short order. Sidewall is the best thing to surround an escaped cat with. He's familiar with it because it is the same material as the tents, and in the hands of men who keep their wits about them and don't frighten the animal, probably scared already in strange surroundings, it can be used like a moving fence until the cage or a shifting den is at hand.

Terrell Jacobs had a bad cat that caught him one afternoon and tore the front out of his uniform. Jacobs fired his revolver, loaded with blanks, straight into the animal's face and drove him off.

An officer of the Society for the Prevention of Cruelty to Animals was nearby—one frequently is during these performances—and he had Jacobs arrested. The powder from a direct blast of a blank gun is bad for the cat's eyes; so usually in an act where the trainer does a lot of shooting, he will point the pistol off to the side of the head and away from the eyes. Jacobs couldn't persuade the officer that the lion had really been trying to get him, but uptown, in the courtroom when he showed his torn costume and scratched chest, the judge fined the lion ten dollars.

During this period Eva and I were doing a popular double "trap" routine and because of the speed and showmanship we put into it we often found that some of our simplest tricks got the biggest hand. After she fell doing the hand-and-foot exchange, we never put that trick back into the act. We finished with a fairly simple but sensational-looking trick called the break-away.

The rigging for this is laced rope that looks like chain and is easily laced. I hung down from the trapeze with the bar under my knees in what is called a hocklock. In my hands I held Eva and around my wrists had the ends of the ropes, the break-away release was controlled by two fingers. The other ends of the chain-woven ropes were looped securely around Eva's ankles. I swung her and suddenly released the finger controls so that she flew out into space toward the spectators. The links of the laced rope disappeared as she traveled in space, but of course the ropes were just the right length to jerk her to a stop with her head a few inches from the ground.

She then would take the loops off her ankles while I unlooped my wrists and dropped the ropes, simultaneously swinging onto my descent rope and sliding to the track where we'd take our bow. We did this finish almost in the time it takes to tell it and I prided myself on the fact that nobody ever beat me to the ground at the end of these turns. I'd come down so fast that I'd wear thin the crotch of my tights and have to have them mended every few days.

Performers alternate their costumes and don't wear the same outfit for two shows in a row. Tights get soaked with perspiration and show dirt from the ropes, and they have to be washed after each use. That's why every day when it's not raining is wash day around a circus and tights are forever waving like a parade of long underwear on clotheslines in every circus back yard.

Eventually I did my act in a sailor costume, even wore an officer's cap which I'd take off when I climbed up into the rigging and don again at the finish of the act in what I thought was a dashing and debonair manner.

Eva was an accomplished aerialist and she didn't like this tour because in the absence of our usual double "trap" act she had little to do in the performance and never got to show off the work she did best. She wanted me to refuse another contract unless it called for our working in the air together instead of my doubling as a clown, but I had been

104

through enough of jumping from one job to another and living in fear of poverty. I was for sticking with the Robinson show come hell or high water, and this led to our first major disagreement.

Since I was still casting around for ways to make more money, I took a shot at the Ringling show where Pat Valdo, a former clown, was in charge of performing personnel. I had an idea that I could do a single and feature the tricky heel catch that I had so much admired in Frank Shepherd's act. Frank did it beautifully, but he never bothered to sell himself —he just came out, did his work in a way to make any aerialist catch his breath, and then came down and walked off with the merest suggestion of a bow.

To do this trick, the performer swings out by his hands from the trapeze bar and lets go, twisting in the air and catching his heels on the swing while it is in motion. Winnie Colleano still does this one beautifully and, like nearly everyone else who does it, works over a net.

I intended to work over a net, but Frank Shepherd never used one. On the Cole Brothers Circus, in 1935, he worked directly over the circular steel arena. If he ever had fallen he would have cut himself in two. He finally made the big-time and wound up doing his act with Ringling Brothers and Barnum & Bailey. It was the finest aerial number in the display, but he worked down in one end of the tent and he still carried it off with so much modesty and so little show-off that people didn't realize how beautiful it was—or how dangerous.

They found out in Akron when this daredevil fell and nearly killed himself. He was crippled for years, but at last got well enough to go into some other kind of business where he is today. A lot of performers come back to circus work from accidents that doctors tell them will force retirement, but Shepherd, tragically enough, was too badly broken.

One of the most versatile performers who ever was in

105

circus business was with the Robinson show in those years—
Walter Guice, who did a spectacular high-bar act. He was a
comedy bareback rider and a ground acrobat, but although
still active under the big top, he has finally given up the stren-
uous work and today is of my pals in clown alley on the
Ringling-Barnum show.

Yet even with the years on him, Walter could never fool
a circus man as to his background. You can look at him and
tell that this man once somersaulted his slim but well-muscled
form from horse to horse and that his good-looking face and
slow smile made many a feminine heart skip a beat when he
looked down into the grandstand from his high bar.

When Walter was riding, I once helped out on a pretty
unethical gag that we framed on him. On an afternoon when it
was time for him to get dressed for his bareback riding turn,
we kept him laughing and talking in the dressing tent until he
lost track of time. Suddenly he heard the band playing his
music. He jumped up and ran for the big top without putting
on his pants, and he was all the way to the entrance before
he discovered it. They had to hold the performance at a stand-
still while he ran back and got dressed. The next day, the
tables turned on me when my tights split mysteriously in an
embarrassing place and exposed me so that I was afraid to
come down out of the rigging and run for the back yard.

In the late summer of 1929, John Robinson's Circus was
showing in South Carolina when word came to the dressing
tent that John Ringling had bought the American Circus Corporation. That included our show along with Sells-Floto,
Hagenbeck-Wallace, Al. G. Barnes and some other properties.

I never had seen John Ringling, but he visited the circus
shortly after this and I met the man who had become the czar
of the big tops on the biggest scale in history. He was tall and
barrel-chested and had long, slim legs, heavy brows and black
hair. John was the only one of the Ringling brothers alive by

this time and his rapidly growing art collection, his oil and railroad interests as well as his circuses had made him one of the best-known, most colorful and respected men in the world.

Eva and I were again doing our double-trapeze act and that night we did our very best. Dressed in white tights and white spangles, we turned in a neat act. Pat Valdo was there with John Ringling and contracted us on the spot for the following season. I had not been clowning nor was I engaged to double in that medium the following season.

Valdo had a quiet manner and a dignified bearing and there was no doubt about his being of Irish extraction. You'd not know it from his last name, which he had changed from Fitzgerald when he started into circus business as a juggler because he thought he would have a better chance if his name sounded as though he had come from some foreign shore.

The Sells-Floto show had Tom Mix for a top feature for the first time in 1929 and he was such a big draw that they say the circus paid for itself between the time John Ringling bought it in late summer until it closed in November. They even had to enlarge the big top to accommodate the crowds. The shows under the new Ringling management all did well that year, but a couple of years later, depression had set in and the big circuses with their heavy operating expense started falling by the wayside. The Robinson show was the first to go. We closed a couple of months before usual "going to bed time" for circuses and it broke our hearts. The "John show," as Robinson's was nicknamed throughout the circus world, was something special. It was the oldest circus on the road and at that time was over one hundred twenty-five years of age. It never went out again, although the Ringling organization still owns the title.

Eva and I were shifted to Sells-Floto, the second biggest circus in the world. It had been the principal competitor of the Ringling Brothers and Barnum & Bailey Circus ever since it had become a success under the management of Bonfils and Tammen of the *Denver Post* some years before.

Quite a few of the old Robinson Circus crowd were with Sells-Floto now and we had a lot of fun that tour. That was the year we organized the Shifters Club. It began one day in Decatur, Illinois, when the lot was a quagmire and we had to "blow" the date after setting up the cookhouse and the horse tents. The lot superintendent quickly saw that the heaviest wagons would mire down and that we never would be able to get the big top into the air. So we all went uptown to the movies while the show was being loaded back onto the railroad cars.

Sitting by the tracks that late afternoon, Bert and Agnes Doss and Eva and I dreamed up the idea of a club in which the first member would pay a one-cent initiation fee, the second member two cents and so on. By the time "Slats" Beason, a tightwire performer, became a member the fee was up to two bucks and he raised hell. So we pegged it at a dollar a head. Thereafter, we added to the treasury by imposing fines for silly infractions such as getting caught talking to any girl on the lot except the wife. We'd hold kangaroo court in the circus back yard between shows, and by the end of the tour we had enough money to throw a big banquet for all members and guests.

Tom Mix was still the foremost feature attraction of Sells-Floto, and he and I became buddies. Tom was a leather craftsman, among other talents, and spent a good deal of his time making fancy belts and harness and pocketbooks. He was a great hand at reciting poetry, too, and he wrote well. He was the first circus performer ever to get ten thousand dollars a week. Out of that, of course, he had to support his troupe of cowboys and cowgirls and the horses, but it was a fabulous piece of change in those days. When he left Sells-

Floto, he started his own circus which lasted only a few years —until Tom was killed in an automobile accident.

Tom was a manly, athletic fellow with hair as black and straight as an Indian's and a jaw that telegraphed to every movie villain that here was a man who would take no foolishness. He liked to have his friends outside the circus business come to travel with him on his handsome private railroad car, but they never stayed long. He was very popular with young America, and the kids would bang on the windows and holler, "Come on out, Tom!" Usually, this was about dawn. Mix was accustomed to it and slept right through, but his guests usually weren't circus people and they just couldn't take it.

Tom spent his money freely, one of his favorite expressions being, "They don't put pockets in shrouds." He didn't take anything with him, but he sure left a lot of friends.

The circus season of 1931 was a rough one for most of the big shows. Even the Ringling outfit closed September 14, the earliest in its history. Sells-Floto was in its final tour, but we didn't know it at the time. The owners decided later that it was not to go out again. The title subsequently was combined with the Al. G. Barnes Circus, but Sells-Floto as such was gone forever.

When we closed in the early autumn of 1931, Eva and I went back to the farm near Mulberry Grove where my mother had remarried. It was quite a reunion, for we hadn't seen our boy for some months. We were just in time to help shuck corn and it felt good to put on old clothes and get out into the fields again. Mother cooked all the things I liked best, especially fried chicken and the kind of corn bread that had been our mainstay when I was a kid on the farm in Missouri. Later on, I used to take the shotgun and go rabbit hunting and Emmett, Jr. would go along. He was old enough to go to school now, walking a mile to the country schoolhouse

109

just as his daddy had done before him. My sister Sylvia was married and living on a farm nearby.

My return to the role of farm boy was all very well for a while, but I had been in another world too long for it to last. I was paying for our board and lodging, but I liked to sit up late and read and listen to the radio, and when I'd oversleep my stepfather would be sore because I wasn't on hand to help with the early morning chores. After Christmas, Eva and I left to fill a winter circus date in Los Angeles and one in Denver, returning to the farm in March. I was beginning to be worried because with the permanent closing of the Sells-Floto Circus I had no contract for the coming circus season.

I'd watch for the rural mailman every day and hurry down to the box. Eva would stand in the yard and day after day I'd have to wave that there wasn't any circus mail. I was reading the *Billboard Magazine* with the circus news in it, the first smells of spring were coming on, and I was a trouper with nothing to troupe with.

At last, desperate, I wired Pat Valdo that I would consider general clowning and that Eva would go into a swinging-ladder act with a girl ensemble. This meant the end of our double-trapeze act and neither of us liked it, but we were in no position to pick and choose. I was running out of money.

I was out in the fields, working, the next day when my mother called to me to come in. "They want you on the telephone at Mulberry Grove," she said. My heart jumped, and I trembled as I picked up the telephone and asked the station agent to read the wire he had for me. "Can place you general clowning on Hagenbeck-Wallace. Advise you contact manager Jess Adkins regarding wife. Possibly he can place her."

Needless to say, I was tremendously relieved. We packed up and took off in our car next day and landed in Peru, Indiana, winter quarters of the Hagenbeck-Wallace Circus. I went immediately to see Adkins and asked him about Eva. "Yes," he said, "we can place her in the ladder act, but her pay will be only eighteen dollars a week."

Adkins, more than any other circus manager I ever saw, looked as the public expects one to look. He was tall and husky, had wavy sandy hair that he let grow a little long in the back. He wore well-tailored suits and a big semi-western hat, and at his vest hung a tiger tooth on a gold watch chain. He wore a diamond ring and a Shrine lapel pin and his hand-made shoes were polished to a mirror finish.

The salary Adkins stated was seven dollars less than Eva had made doing an ensemble number before, and my pay for clowning was only thirty-five bucks, but we were glad to get it. I worked in whiteface and one of my "walk-arounds" occurred to me when I passed a junky-looking shop and noticed a big, stuffed bullfrog in the window. I bought him and applied some bright paint so he would look shiny. I fitted him to a skullcap and wore him on my head while I walked around looking for him, a lantern in one hand and a gig in the other. That season, I played a battered bass horn in Earl Shipley's clown band. The street parades had been discontinued some years before, but we still had the clown band—now for a ring number. Shipley played trombone and directed the band. When we had staggered through a murderous "classical" rendition and it was time for the trombone to hit a very low note, Shipley would keep trying for it to no avail. Finally the tuba player in the regular circus band would hit it for him. The gag always drew laughs.

Clyde Beatty was with us that year, as in previous tours. He had been an absolute sensation in Madison Square Garden, where he appeared in the Ringling-Barnum show during its New York City engagement, and then returned to us inasmuch as our opening date was later than Ringling's.

In an Indiana city, I was in the dressing tent and it seemed to me that the band would never stop playing the

111

music for the wild animal act. I did not know until a few moments later that one of Clyde's tigers had gone to work on him. The first I knew of it was when I started for the big top to make my first clown entrance and saw him being carried out, blood all over his pants.

Inside the steel arena the cats were being driven back into the chutes and it was a wild scramble, for they were bloodthirsty and confused. A tiger had gone for the trainer, tearing the chair from his hand, when Clyde slipped and fell to one knee. The weight of the striped giant kept him from getting back on his feet and it looked as if he would be clawed and chewed to death before the men outside the big cage could get to him. Then a male lion had leaped off his pedestal and attacked the tiger, taking his attention from Clyde. While the big cats went round and round, he had staggered to his feet and escaped through the safety door. The attendants had a time trying to separate the lion and the tiger with prodding poles and blank cartridge fire, and there was the danger that other animals—there were nearly forty in the cage—would join in the melee. The audience was on the verge of panic, too, but somehow order was restored when the equestrian director's whistle blew, and the next acts went on as though nothing had happened.

Beatty was badly hurt, but nobody realized that night how close he was to dying. Clyde had "jungle fever" and when it was discovered next day, he was rushed to a hospital at Indianapolis where luckily a rare but vital serum was available. The newspapers screamed the story for days and the publicity was great for the circus when he came back and went into the big cage again with that mixed group of snarling devils. But it was a mighty near thing and the circus people knew that all the newspaper stories could have been a simple obituary instead.

There was a special angle to the story because the lion had attacked the tiger and got him off the trainer in time to

112

save his life. All the stories played up the fact that this big male lion loved Clyde and had come to his rescue. Beatty was smart enough to play along with this, but privately he grinned and said he figured the lion hated the tiger and had been waiting for a good chance to go for him when he was "busy."

I was carrying our trapeze rigging along with me that year, thinking that Eva and I might be called upon in an emergency, but it never happened. Eva was unhappy at not being in a principal act, but there was nothing I could do about it. This was depression time and we were lucky to be working at all. Lots of circus performers were unable to find the sort of thing they had been trained for and were working in hot-dog joints, filling stations and anywhere else they could be paid. Hagenbeck-Wallace showed a profit that year and it was pretty certain that the show would take the road again in 1933. When, toward the end of the tour, I was offered a contract for the next year, I signed it even though it did not provide for us to go back to double trapeze.

I did some serious thinking that winter and decided that if I was going to have to spend all my time in clown alley, I would not be just another clown, but would try to improve my work and create something special. The sad little tramp was nudging my mind again and I finally made up my mind that, win or lose, I would bring him to life under the big top. So when Hagenbeck-Wallace opened in 1933, I said goodbye to whiteface clowning for good and all. And I never went back to it except once when I had to commit a murder. But that's another story.

Fame is nothing more than a place in history and in the mouths of people who talk. It satisfies vanity, but only occasionally brings bread.

Dan Rice

BIGGER AND BETTER

The Hagenbeck-Wallace Circus in 1933 was a great organization. We had Clyde Beatty for a top feature and the publicity from his close call the season before made him one of the great names of the entertainment world. Courtney Riley Cooper wrote him up in the major magazines and Edward Anthony wrote his book, *The Big Cage*. A motion picture had been made under the same title and was being released in the spring of our tour.

Our wild-animal menagerie was now so extensive that we had to use a nine-pole tent to exhibit it. The Poodles Hanneford bareback-riding act was with the show and the Clarkonians were one of the flying-trapeze acts. Rudy Rudynoff had the principal liberty-horse act, and there was an East Indian named "Bombayo" who did a startling act on a bounding rope. Also, we had one of the "giraffe-neck women" from upper Burma. Three had been imported by the Ringling organization which placed two on the Ringling-Barnum Circus and gave one to us. These women had necks elongated since early childhood by the placing of brass rings around them—pushing up the neck until at maturity it was fully a foot in length. There was some religious meaning to it, or perhaps it was just a beauty treatment like the saucer lips of the Ubangi Savages from French Equatorial Africa, who were a feature of the Ringling show in 1930 and again in 1932. Anyhow, our giraffe-neck girl, whose name was Mu Kau, was a real educational novelty and our publicity department made the most of it—even to taking her to the Smithsonian Institute in Washington, D.C., for the inspection of the eminent anthropologist, Ales Hrdlicka.

That year the Hagenbeck-Wallace Circus route included such big stands as Chicago, Philadelphia, Washington, Baltimore and New York City where we set up the tents opposite the Yankee Stadium.

I never had been on Manhattan Island, but I had seen the skyline during a previous tour that took in some New Jersey territory. While we were in the "big apple," as show folk call New York City, I went to old man Guttenberg's place. He dealt in antiquated show costumes and there I spotted a brown derby with black splotches. I knew instantly I had to have it for my tramp clown characterization which up to this point had lacked a finishing touch. The price was a dollar and it was the greatest bargain of my career, for I am still wearing that hat. I have had it rebuilt, papier-mâchéd inside and otherwise repaired through the years. The circus museum at Sarasota, Florida, has asked for it and that is its probable destination unless I lose it some night in a windstorm or unless it is stolen.

This was the year that beer came back so I thought up a topical clown gag about it. I bought a big stone jar and had two holes drilled in it for a rope handle. It was so heavy I had to build a prop box to carry it in, and then pad the box against breaking the jar. I got a bunch of beer-bottle caps and strung them over one arm. In one hand I carried some empty beer bottles and in the other a capping lever. On the crock I

116

painted HOME BREW OUTFIT FOR SALE CHEAP. It got a lot of laughs that season.

I used the frog-hunting gag, too, only now in my tramp characterization, and with Otto Griebling I worked up what is called a progressive clown stunt. Otto works in a sort of tramp clown makeup, but he is short, blond and stocky and we don't look at all alike. From the pop stand each day we would get a twenty-five pound cake of ice. Early in the performance, we would circle the hippodrome track with me carrying the ice on my back and Otto calling into the seats for "Missus Jones" who was supposed to have ordered the ice. We came back three or four times in the course of the performance, each time the ice block considerably melted until on the last trip I was licking a little ice cube and Otto was still calling hopefully for "Missus Jones."

During this tour, I drew a cartoon of our feature acts which the press department used widely as a two-column cut. I had kept busy with my pen in spare moments, for still I had an undercurrent of desire for cartooning. Now that the sad little hobo had jumped from paper and ink to flesh and blood, I dreamed of using him in a comic strip one day. Even today he has not yet achieved this immortality, but he is still dreaming.

Our manager, Jess Adkins, was always wanting to revive the circus street parade, absent from circus day for a number of years. To prove that the revival of the "march" would be good for publicity and, consequently, for business, he put a test parade together in St. Louis, later in a New Jersey town and, finally, in Cleveland where no circus had paraded for fourteen years. This procession turned the town upside down. More than a hundred thousand people lined the sidewalks. Business was good and everybody was happy except the street cleaners. We had twenty-eight elephants with Hagenbeck-Wallace that year and over one hundred horses. Adkins was

117

a real showman who believed in giving the people something for their money.

"Cheerful" Gardner, a great elephant man who got his nickname because of his dour, Scottish disposition, was in charge of our "ponderous pachyderms." He had one old girl who was trained to lie down in traffic. The publicity department pretended that she was a victim of sudden vertigo or fainting spells. She would lie down in front of a streetcar or a line of automobile traffic and refuse to get up until "Cheerful" gave her the signal. Meanwhile, cars were jammed for blocks, cops were driven half crazy and newspaper photographers had pictures—which was the main idea.

During all this tour, the double-trapeze rigging was still packed away and my mind was on making something special out of my tramp clown character. My wife was still working in the aerial ensemble numbers, but nowhere was her talent used to its full extent and she was unhappy. Also, we were not making as much money as we had made when we had done an aerial act together, and I couldn't blame her for being upset about it. I was unwilling to leave the security of a full-season circus job in order to book our old double-trap act elsewhere. This was what really broke up our marriage, this "professional" bickering. There never was any question of either of us being in love with anyone else. It was just one of those unfortunate things that happen to show folks which people outside this crazy business never can understand.

Eva had maintained that she never would troupe again unless we were booked together in the air, but by the end of that 1933 tour she was pregnant and we both knew she would be unable to go with a circus by the time the next spring season rolled around.

I clowned some winter circus dates in Detroit, Cleveland, Minneapolis and St. Paul, making about fifty dollars a week, although out of that I had to pay my board and room. The

118

traveling circus always furnished meals and of course we slept on the train. Late in the winter, I had a letter from Adkins saying that the makeshift street parades the year before had proved so successful that he had persuaded the Ringling Organization that Hagenbeck-Wallace should reinstate the "march" as a daily feature of the 1934 tour. He wanted me to come to winter quarters and do the "art work" on some of the tableau wagons.

Soon I was busy with an armful of fairy-tale books from the public library, a lot of brushes and paints and five circus wagons with a total of ten sides to illustrate. This was a chance to show what the clown could do as an artist. I used the Red Riding Hood theme, Peter Pumpkin Eater, Popeye, the Three Bears, Mary and Her Lamb and then I went modern and copied Walt Disney's mouse people in a panel entitled "Mouseville." This proved to be the most popular wagon of all. They all were destined for the street parade and were wagons in which props and other things were regularly carried. By parade time, they were emptied and sent into the street parade purely for their "artistic" value in contrast to the "practical" units with open cages and wagons with bands playing on top.

I had the modesty to paint "With apologies to Walt Disney" on the mouse unit before I signed my name. When Jess Adkins noted that I had put my signature on every panel, I overheard him say to Ernie Sylvester, the boss painter of the Hagenbeck-Wallace show, "Well, I see that Kelly sure believes in signing his name." Without saying anything, I painted out all the signatures except the Disney line and reduced my name to very small letters.

On the "Mouseville" wagon, I painted one side to show mouse people looking at a circus poster which advertised "Felix the Cat's Combined Shows." The panel contained all sorts of "citizens" including mouse mothers with baby carriages filled with lively little offspring. The other side illustrated the arrival of Felix's circus. The cat was busy doing everything—putting up the big top, carrying flapjacks for the cookhouse, leading elephants and selling popcorn.

I was putting the finishing touches on this one when Ernie yelled to me that I was wanted on the telephone. It was a call from the hospital. "You are the father of a baby boy and your wife is doing fine," the voice on the other end of the wire informed me.

I hurried to the hospital and there met Thomas Patrick Kelly, our second son. He was small—weighing into this busy world at six pounds, but perfect in all ways and not as yet making any special fuss about being born the son of a clown.

During that season of 1934 I rode a tiny bicycle in the street parade. It was a child size and geared so that I had to pedal fast to keep up with the "march." Actually, I could make much better time than the tempo of the other parade units and I took full advantage of it. My position was behind the calliope where "Crazy Ray" played steam music in the old tradition from a beautifully carved wagon that has now become a museum piece. But I would pedal forward to the very front of the parade where our dignified equestrian director, Harry MacFarland, was riding in an open buggy drawn by fine, high-stepping hackneys. Having achieved this forward position and gained considerable time, I would duck into a saloon and have a quick beer and then catch the tail end of the parade. Sometimes I would blow my breath at MacFarland just to make him envious.

Our show that year made more money than the Ringling Circus by the time we closed on a chill late-autumn day in Dixie, but earlier in the fall we had some unexpected excitement in Richmond, Virginia. I was busy at the circus electric-light plant at parade time, borrowing a little oil for my bicycle, and the parade was lined up in the street when somebody came running along shouting, "Get a piece of sidewall; get a piece of sidewall!"

I know right away that one of the big cats was loose and that they wanted sidewall to corral him with. A moment later, when I looked toward the ticket wagon, I saw Earl Lindsay, the treasurer, coming out with an automatic rifle in his hand.

The next thing I saw was a groom leading a pair of baggage horses back to the horse tents and away from the parade lineup. One horse which later had to be shot had his nose ripped to ribbons. The bolt on the door of a lion den had jarred loose when the cage was being pulled into line over rough pavement and had swung open. A lion had jumped out onto the street and the first thing he had done was to attack one of the horses hitched to the cage. A lion on the loose is most apt to attack a zebra or a horse, since they are the natural food of the big cats.

The lion was shot in the flank by a policeman after he had slashed the horse. Then he started limping along the "line of march" until he saw the open door of a tin shop. He went in while the men working there ran out the back door and slammed it shut. Then one of them with courage and quick thinking ran around to the front door and closed it. Adkins and Beatty and the circus vet looked in the window at the cat. The bullet had hit an artery and they decided it was no use to try to save him, so they gave the signal to a cop to finish him off.

After all this excitement, the parade moved on as usual and none of the spectators downtown knew anything unusual had happened until they read the home edition of the evening papers. To the circus people, it was simply another "fact of life in show business" and I guess the only remarkable thing about these things is that they don't happen more often.

That winter I worked up a drawing act and got my first bookings into night clubs. Some of the dates worried me because the drunks were so loud and objectionable, but a clown pal of mine named "Kinko," who had an act that worked a week ahead of me on the circuit, convinced me that I could ignore them. "Forget the drunks," he said. "There will always be enough sober patrons to appreciate your act." My act was the old chalk-talk, embellished with some new props and art work and presented by the tramp clown instead of by a guy playing straight.

This was the winter when, during a circus engagement for the Shrine in Detroit, I tried out the PWA "shovel" routine that rocketed to national fame. In this gag, Otto Griebling was the boss on the job and carried blueprints and stakes and measuring tape. I was his worker and of course I was "Weary Willie." Otto scurried around and staked out a plot while I just stood still and looked world-weary and leaned on a shovel. The leaning on the shovel caught the fancy of a member of the Republican committee in Detroit and he had us photographed. It was a popular picture and its circulation was nationwide. A lot of Roosevelt Democrats took offense, but the circus got plenty of publicity and it had been conceived as an innocent, non-political gag. On this same order, in the spring of 1953, I departed from my traditional derby hat for one walk-around in which I wore a black Homburg and carried a battered golf bag to show how our President's hobby might evoke the interest of even a hobo. It got a good laugh and I like to think that "Ike" would have laughed loudest of all if he had seen it.

A milestone in the circus business occurred in the winter of 1934-35. Jess Adkins and Zack Terrell, who had been the manager of the defunct Sells-Floto show, got together and put out a show of their own. Its title was Cole Brothers and Clyde Beatty Combined Circus—Clyde was a partner. I elected to put in with this new outfit, but Eva would not go along since we were not booked for our double-trapeze act. I sent her money throughout that tour, but it was becoming apparent that our marriage was falling apart.

Early in the 1935 season, I was in Kokomo, Indiana, when a man came back to the dressing tent and asked for me. He wore street clothes, but flashed a badge and said, "I am the sheriff of Howard County and I have an attachment on your trunk and on your body for appearance in court. Do you know what this is?"

I told him that I could make a pretty good guess. He laughed and said, "You aren't the first poor devil I have had to do this to."

That Eva wanted a divorce came as no surprise, but I could not wait to appear in court and let the circus go on without me. Jess Adkins didn't want me to leave the show and suggested I get an attorney to handle it all for me. Clyde Beatty and I had joined the Elks together and I recalled that one of the members who had been very friendly was an attorney. He took the case and wired me later when it came up. I did not contest it in any way. Even though I realized this meant the end of our differences I was far from happy or in any way lighthearted about it.

We had agreed in advance that we would each take the responsibility of one son. I was to take the older one. Of course I couldn't take him with me on the circus except for brief periods when he was not required to go to public school, but my sister Sylvia and her husband volunteered to take him and he grew up in Lafayette, Indiana. He did a hitch in the United States Navy during the war and now works for the Chesapeake and Ohio—a railroader like his grandfather.

Eva eventually married a circus clown named Joe Lewis, and she still does aerial work. Our paths have crossed a few times and the meetings have always been friendly. Because the kind of traveling I have had to do while making a living permitted me so little home life, my boys grew up without

123

getting to know their pop very well and now even Tommy is a full-size man. There is no surer way of realizing how fast time goes than to have kids you must be away from for long periods. I lost track of time as I did the same things in the same ways on the same show in town after town across the country and back, but my feeling that time was somehow standing still was busted wide open every time I'd get back to see my boys and find them changed in size and manner. They are fine boys, but none of the credit for their raising, I regret to say, is due to me.

After the divorce, I became melancholy for long periods and this feeling worked its way inevitably into Kelly, the clown. With my family scattered, I had only the sad-faced hobo and we became at this time indistinguishable.

I was determined to make something of myself through this character. I went into twelve or fifteen numbers twice a day six days a week. I wanted to appear so often that the hobo would be nailed down in the minds of the spectators. I did everything I could think of in contrasts. Where other clowns were white and neat, I was unshaven and ragged. They were active; I gave the appearance of doing almost nothing, and what I did accomplish was geared to a tempo so relaxed that it would make a snail seem jet-propelled.

During this period I put the finishing touches on several of my routines including the soulful stare I'd level at lady spectators while I nibbled on wisps of leaves from a big head of cabbage. I got so I could sort out from the mass of faces in the circus grandstand the kind of women who would find this harmless clowning irresistibly funny. And sometimes I would work it on some over-dignified woman if only to amuse her escort.

I worked up another stunt in which I carried a long board and a saw. It sounds ridiculous, but when I would slant the board into the seats and practically stick it under people's

124

noses and start sawing as though what I had to do was so terribly important that I didn't even notice they were there, it got real belly laughs. Later, I varied it and added a blueprint which I pretended to follow. It developed into a variation of the old WPA job that Otto Griebling and I had done years earlier.

Cracking a peanut with a sledge hammer and looking heartbroken when nothing is left of it but fine powder is a routine that came by accident. Sometimes kids in the stands feel sorry for me and offer me candy and other things to eat. One day a boy handed me a peanut. I took it and pretended it was so hard I couldn't bite into the shell or break it in my hands. I looked around for something and saw a sledge hammer leaning against a clump of stakes to which some aerial rigging had been fastened. I carried it back to the seats and on one of the posts of the iron railing that separates the first rows of seats from the hippodrome track I gingerly cracked the peanut. The sledge was so heavy that just tapping the nut left almost nothing and then I pretended to be sadder than ever. It was so effective immediately that I still use it today.

A lot of other clown laughs are born accidentally and some of the stuff we plan carefully and expect to send folks into gales of laughter doesn't come off at all. There is a kind of three-way rule to clowning as I do it. I must suit the action to the mood and to the makeup and everyone of these is exaggerated. I am sure that it scarcely sounds funny in print. Telling it here does it an injustice because it lacks the important dimension of seeing the clown makeup.

I am a sad and ragged little guy who is very serious about everything he attempts—no matter how futile or how foolish it appears to be. I am the hobo who found out the hard way that the deck is stacked, the dice "frozen," the race fixed and the wheel crooked, but there is always present that one tiny, forlorn spark of hope still glimmering in his soul which

125

makes him keep on trying. All I can say beyond that is that there must be a lot of people in this world who feel that way and that, fortunately, they come to the circus. In my tramp clown character, folks who are down on their luck, have had disappointments and have maybe been pushed around by circumstances beyond their control, see a caricature of themselves. By laughing at me, they really laugh at themselves, and realizing that they have done this gives them a sort of spiritual second wind for going back into the battle.

I never talk to spectators and I never laugh. I have heard men lay some substantial bets with each other on the subject of making me laugh, but the ones who bet on the laugh never had much fun out of it, and even less profit.

During the winter of 1936-37 I was doing my cartoon act in night clubs. A booker named Pete Iodice caught the act and liked it, and after that, I had just about all the work I could do.

In the spring of 1937, the Cole Brothers and Clyde Beatty Combined Circus dared to invade the very center of New York City, long the exclusive stamping ground of the Ringling Brothers and Barnum & Bailey show. We put our circus into the old Hippodrome on Sixth Avenue between 43rd and 44th Streets. The show was wonderfully well received by the New York press and radio writers, but the larger Ringling show a few blocks away in its traditional Madison Square Garden setting did the business.

During this engagement I started going with a girl who worked for the Hippodrome at one of the refreshment stands out in the foyer where she picked up a lot of conversation from customers. From her I learned that I was getting over very well. She heard Brooks Atkinson, the critic of the *New York Times,* predict one evening, while having a sandwich, that the Ringling show would hire me away from Cole Brothers and that one day my ragged clothes, battered derby, putty nose and tramp makeup would be famous.

When we were showing that summer in New Haven, Connecticut, the word was flashed in the dressing tent that a show owner from England was in the seats watching our matinee. I spotted him immediately when I did my first walk-around. He was handsome, dressed in a dignified manner and had his Homburg hat parked on an empty chair beside him. With him was an attractive blond woman who I learned later was his wife.

I did the peanut gag with the sledge hammer right in front of him, but the hammer slipped off the rail and flattened his hat. It was not harmed and he smiled and picked it up without paying much attention to me. His attention was all for the liberty-horse acts that were working in the rings. But the woman with him was laughing and nudging him to pay attention to me as I wandered away to perform for another group around the big oval. In subsequent appearances that afternoon, I finally managed to catch this important-looking man's interest. When the afternoon show had ended and I went to the dressing room to wash up, a lot of the guys were kidding about who was going to England. "By golly," said MacFarland, "I bet that Britisher is here to steal people away from this show!"

All this time the distinguished-looking stranger was standing by my trunk. He must have heard all the talk about him in the confusion of the "alley," but he gave no sign of being ill at ease. He asked me if I was Mr. Kelly, and I told him that I was. "My name is Bernard Mills and I am from the Bertram Mills Circus in England," he said. "May I have a word with you?"

This man was a member of the principal circus family of the world outside the United States. I invited him to sit

127

down in the dressing tent, but he declined to discuss business there. "I will wait for you in the stables," he said.

When I was cleaned up, I found Bernard Mills talking with the grooms and looking over our ring stock. "Mr. Kelly," he began, "my business is this: we have a Christmas show which begins about the nineteenth of December and runs for six weeks in a large building and I want to know if you would be interested in working that engagement."

This was a chance to appear with the famous Bertram Mills London Olympia show and I did not stall around. "I think I can go," I told him. "I haven't signed a contract with anyone for next winter as yet; yes, I think I could make it. How much are you paying?"

He explained, in pound sterling, then worth $4.74, that he would pay me a certain salary plus my transportation over and back. "I will be back to see you when your show exhibits in Springfield, Massachusetts, in a few days and I will bring a contract with me." With that, he shook hands, bowed formally and walked away.

Walking on air, I went back to the dressing tent, where the guys gave me a big send-off because I was the only member of the circus who had been chosen.

I lived in the clouds for the next few days until the circus landed in Springfield where Bernard Mills was due to show up with my contract. We had a pouring rain most of that day and I became discouraged. No Mills; no contract. Was he just kidding? Finally, I spotted him wading through the menagerie tent and I headed him off. "Mr. Kelly," he began, "I came to tell you that I haven't had time to make out your contract, but I will mail it to you before I go to Canada."

I figured that this might be a kiss-off, but a few days later there was a man waiting for me on the lot with a big brown envelope that had come special delivery by registered mail. It was the contract. I signed it and sent one copy to

128

England. In San Antonio, that autumn, I had my passport photo taken. Then, when the circus closed, I hurried to Indiana to see my son and my sister and her husband. I then went to New York, picked up my steamship tickets and visited the British consul for my visa. I had to have my mother sign an affidavit to account for my birth date. There was no record to be had back in the town where I was born.

All that summer circus tour, I had been writing to the girl I had dates with during the Hippodrome engagement. She liked me enough to hint that she'd like me to take her to Europe, but I was "gun-shy" and hadn't recovered from the hurt of the marriage that had busted up.

In New York, I was told that the ship I was going over on was the same size as the *Deutschland,* so I went down to look at that one for comparison. This was all quite a thrill for me because the farm boy never had been to sea. Later I boarded my ship, was shown to my stateroom and was assigned a seat in the dining room. Then I went up on deck. This was my thirty-eighth birthday, but there wasn't a soul there I knew. By midnight, when I felt the ship moving, there had been parties with bands and confetti. Still, I was "the little man who wasn't there." I was suddenly homesick for the farm, for my folks, for the friends of the big top. In all the departing excitement there had been nobody to say, "Happy Birthday, Emmett." If I had been wearing my ragged wardrobe and the hobo makeup, I probably could not have looked more forlorn.

I was leaning on the rail, looking at the disappearing skyline of Manhattan when a voice called, "Kelly, what are you doing here?" It was Karl Wallenda of the high-wire act. With him were two girls I had known in indoor circuses, all headed to play in Berlin for a few weeks. I felt wonderful right away and we drank Bock beer and sat up half the night talking about old times.

Next morning the ship was rolling so that I could hardly

129

shave. The man who shared my cabin was a German-born American from Milwaukee who was on his way back to see his family. He ate a hearty breakfast while I bravely ordered grapefruit and ham and eggs and coffee. I managed to get the grapefruit down, but the sight of the main course sent me to my stateroom for three days.

When I felt better, I sat in a deck chair with a blanket over me and breathed the stimulating salt air, but the Germans walking by with their big pipes and cigars would make me sick all over again. One afternoon a fellow introduced himself to me and explained that he too was going to the Bertram Mills engagement and that he was contracted to appear in the side show. His specialty was being able to contain a lot of golf balls in his mouth. After he'd crammed them all in and then removed them, he would say to the spectators: "Silly, isn't it? But it's better than work!" When he asked me what I did for a living, I told him I just looked sad at people.

One night on that first crossing, the engines stopped and the sudden quiet woke me up. The steward told me that a man had jumped overboard. They couldn't see him, but they threw life preservers overboard in all directions—the kind with torches on them that light up when they hit the water. The ship circled for three hours and gave up the search.

On a December morning we landed at Cherbourg. Sea gulls and fishing boats and hills made a picture that I'll long remember. In Southampton, I got into a minor jam with the customs officer who said that the three pairs of leather shoes, pocketbook and stockings I was taking to Rose Behee who was already in England with the flying trapeze act and wanting these things, were in violation of the customs rules. First he told me to throw them in the water; then he relented and said: "Oh, well, because it's almost Christmas I'll let it go by."

At Waterloo Station an old man with a wheelbarrow

handled my trunk for me. I got into a cab on a misty, cold day and felt miserable and lonely again. I had lost Karl Wallenda and the girls and now knew nobody but a golf-ball side-show guy with whom I had agreed to share a room in London. My trunk and I were dumped off at a monstrous, glass-domed building where I reported to Miss Moore, secretary to Mr. Mills.

She gave me the address of my "digs" and I went there, but I did not like the meager accommodations. A bed and one chair, pitcher and bowl, a meter into which you could drop a shilling and get some heat, and a gas light, was about all there was to it. I ordered beer in the bar, but it was bitter and warm. Finally, I found some German imported beer and it tasted wonderful. The sandwiches were cold, the meat pies were cold, the weather was cold—nothing warm but the beer. In reality, I had nothing much to complain about. It was simply a matter of adjustment and circus people who come to our country for the first time probably have just as much trouble and feel just as lonely.

The side-show man liked our "digs" well enough, but I moved next morning to a hotel called the Kensington. This was a comfortable, friendly place with a good pub and a snack bar that stayed open late. I would buy shrimp in a fish market and carry them to the bar after the show to eat with the beer. The bartender noted this and when I returned to that place after an absence of nine years and a world war, his word of greeting was, "Where's the bag of shrimp?"

The building in which Bertram Mills presented the London Olympia Circus was so huge that the circus was only one, although the main, attraction. In another area there was laid out a regular county fair midway (all under a roof) with two Ferris wheels, merry-go-rounds, a caterpillar ride, three whips, many side shows and concession stands. It was the biggest thing of its kind I ever had seen.

131

I was in time for rehearsals and on that second visit to the building met Frank Foster, the ringmaster, and Jack Lindsey, the band leader. They and all the other Britishers were wonderful to me. They made sure my dressing room was comfortable and they introduced me around. Show folks are the same everywhere. It is a great fraternity—all classes, all colors, all religions, all nationalities, and all for the show. They work too hard and share too many dangers to spend their time fighting. They are a sort of United Nations, all dedicated to the single purpose of "keeping the show on the road."

The Mills indoor circus at the Olympia was a one-ringer with wide aisles and good seating and with about three feet of space between the ring perimeter and the first row of boxes. Their acts were all feature attractions—none of what we call "standard acts" or fill-ins to pad out the performance, and while the acts are permitted to take their time and show their skill to best advantage, the shifting of props and everything pertaining to transition is lightning-fast. This circus wants its acts to present only their best tricks and not waste time with "warm-up" turns. The band plays familiar circus music, but it was strange to me to hear fiddles and piano in that band, since we use no strings in American circus bands.

I was getting more nervous by the hour. Bernard Mills had a brother named Cyril and I had been tipped off through the famous circus "grapevine," which for some unaccountable reason seems to work faster than a jet plane, that Cyril had raised hell with his brother for hiring me. "A ragged hobo clowning in the Bertram Mills Circus! Impossible!" is the gist of how he is reported to have reacted to the news that Bernard had signed a contract with me.

I had no idea how the Britishers would like my work. Before the start of the circus performance, they lit up the ring bright as a new dollar. I peeked through the curtain and saw

132

a great bank of formal evening clothes—gowns and stiff-shirt fronts, monocles and lorgnettes and opera glasses. The Lord Mayor of London was in his box. My first routine would precede the official circus opening by the few minutes in which I would pretend to sweep the ring, slapping with my old broom at a little pool of light that kept tagging my steps. Of course it was a spotlight and I never could catch it. This was a variation on a routine that little "Shorty" Flemm used to do as a preliminary to the beginning of the Ringling-Barnum Circus in Madison Square Garden. "Shorty" dressed as an elderly rube comic for this one. Doing a clown number before the show starts officially is called "working the come-in" because at this time people are still coming into the seats.

Well, I peeked through that curtain separating the American clown from his foreign audience and my knees shook. But I had a round-trip ticket. The worst they could do was cancel me and ship me home. So I worked the "come-in" and after the spotlight routine I added a little bit in which I blew up a balloon until it broke, looked woe-begone and heartbroken when it burst; then made a little grave for it and buried it as a child would a shattered toy. The pathetic quality I put into that bit must have been authentic because it got over very well.

Now I had a little more courage. The circus started. I saw Cyril Mills in the family box—white tie and tails and a stop-watch in his hand. Very distinguished in appearance and all business. For my first walk-around, they told me to use a loaf of bread instead of the head of cabbage. I started nibbling in front of Kay Stammers, the British tennis champion, and as I sat down in front of her and stared like a bum who had fallen hopelessly in love with a princess, nibbling on the bread all the while, she almost went into hysterics. Whether it was because she was a good actress and sensed perhaps that I needed help at this point or whether it really amused her that

133

much I'll never know. Anyhow, I will always remember Kay Stammers, for out of the corner of my eye I could see Cyril Mills smiling a little at what had been going on between the tennis champion and the hobo comic.

Later I felt somebody tugging at my elbow and it was Bertram Mills himself, the father of Bernard and Cyril and the real head of the show. "Mr. Kelly," he whispered, "when you get to the Lord Mayor, offer him a piece of bread, too."

I did as he told me and it went over very well. In fact, by the end of the performance I was "in," as we say in the amusement business. The *London Mirror* next day carried a picture of Kay Stammers and me and the cut-lines or text had to do with "the loafer with the loaf—the American hobo comedian who brought a new kind of clowning to Bertram Mills Olympia last night."

That first night I had worked as never before—all over the theatre and clear up into the top balcony where the folks sat who could not afford the top-price seats. I was bone-weary when it was all over, but I went to the Kensington bar and grill with some of the American acts like the golf-ball guy, Bob Mathews and his wife, Gertrude, who had a lion act in the show. And I was happy.

I got to love that friendly little hotel, but when I returned to London in 1947 I was shocked and saddened by what had happened during the blitz. The newsstand and drugstore were gone and the front was all boarded up. Only the pub remained. The wife of the man tending bar—the fellow who had made the crack about the shrimp—showed me around inside. The roof had caved in; only a couple of rooms remained. The Olympia building itself had suffered some damage, but not too much for quick repair. A light bomb had hit in the courtyard near the power plant and the concussion had shattered a lot of glass. This had been replaced. But I am getting ahead of my story.

134

That first time in London, we had opened the circus engagement on December 20. I planned to spend Christmas Day in the English countryside that I had heard so much about. I wanted to make a trip of about one hundred miles by train and bus. And I planned to make it alone so there would be no distractions. My decision to duck all Christmas invitations boomeranged on me, for the day was so thick with yellow fog that you could almost write your name on it. I sat around the hotel most of the day, and when I did venture out I was as lost in a minute as a Montana rancher who can't find his way back from the barn to his house in a snowstorm. I felt my way along by keeping my hand on the walls until I got to the Addison Road Station, which was lit up. I knew my way from there and finally the country boy from Kansas and Missouri found his way home.

I found the British audiences a little slower to respond, for they seem to study the acts more. But once they make up their minds about you, they are not fickle and restless and forever demanding that you change your routines. They like you to do the things that caught their fancy the first time they saw you, and they are generous with their applause.

A clown laugh, as a matter of fact, is a laugh in any language because it is in pantomime. Anyone can understand sign language and that is essentially what it is. In the days of the one-ring circuses in America, we had what were called "talking clowns." They cracked jokes, sang comedy songs, carried on a running-fire feud with the ringmaster and even recited passages of Shakespeare. Their origin was Europe, of course. In the old country, the circuses stayed one-ringers for the most part, but in America the tents spread out and we soon had three-ring performances in tents so large that the old-style talking and singing clown had to change his tactics. He returned to the clown fundamental—pantomime. He lost something, too, because clowning became merely part of a fast-paced pattern and no longer rated the attention that, say, Dan Rice and some other noted talking clowns commanded in the days between the Civil War and the 'eighties when the circuses began to take on considerable size. No less a circus man than P. T. Barnum once remarked that "Clowns are pegs used to hang circuses on," but from the days of Dan Rice— a contemporary and friend of Abraham Lincoln—until now, I do not know of any circus featuring its clowns individually in newspaper advertisements or in posters. It seems that when the clown lost his voice in this business he lost his billing, too.

The most famous British clown was Joseph Grimaldi, but he worked in theatres and music halls, not in the circus at any time. Charles Dickens wrote a book about Grimaldi which had quite a success. Even though he never was a circus clown, the circus clowns in America long ago appropriated a piece of Grimaldi's front name for a sobriquet. We all call ourselves "joeys" in honor of this great clown.

This story has been told before, but as long as we are on the subject of Joe Grimaldi, I want to set it down again. Grimaldi, in his later years, became depressed and ill and without telling his name sought the services of a well-known doctor. "You need to laugh more and relax," the doctor told him. "I recommend that you go regularly to the theatre and pay special attention to a comedian named Grimaldi."

The clowns with the Mills show were fine folks. I used to enjoy watching a clown act named Coco, Percy and Alby Austin do what is called the "water entry." It is pure Huckster slapstick and the crowd loves it. Perfect timing was required as this trio climbed stepladders with buckets of water, spilled it, fell into it and sloshed it around on each other—that is all but Percy, dressed in immaculate evening dress. He was so skillful that he never got wet at all, though everybody was waiting for the "toff" to get it good. The act wound up in a tussle, and then a well-dressed man would step out from the audience to break it up and fall into a tub of water for a finish gag.

Olympia had an eighty-year-old clown named Joe Craston who did nothing but go up into the seats with his pet dog under his arm and shake hands with children. They had "Lulu," one of the few women ever to clown with a circus, in the "joey" department and she later spent two seasons with the Ringling Brothers and Barnum & Bailey Circus. Mills had a French clown, too. All these people were extremely pleasant to me, and we were competitive neither as to makeup nor styles of clowning.

Nothing ran fast in London except the trains and the circus performance. The thing I liked best about the town was its tempo. Everything was slower. I loved to just walk around and look into the chemists' shops, the places of the iron-mongers, the fish markets and the trinket places. The shops of the chemists still had old-fashioned colored-water bottles and they smelled of drugs—not cooked grease. In England a boy who wanted to be a pharmacist didn't flunk the course if he couldn't learn to make sandwiches.

The Mills people I found to be dignified, fair, intelligent and generous, and they are a credit to the business. The late Bertram Mills gave me a nice surprise one afternoon when I was clowning in the seats of the top balcony. The lights suddenly blacked out and I heard somebody singing, "Has anybody here seen Kelly?" Then a spotlight started searching for me and eventually caught me with my loaf of bread, nibbling at it and staring sadly at a woman spectator.

When I returned to ring level, Mr. Bertram stopped me and said, "How did you like my song?" I hadn't realized until then that the boss of the show himself had thought up this thing and put it into motion.

"I thought it was wonderful," I told him.

"Well, he said, "I can't be here to do it every day, but I'll have Alby Austin, the clown, sing it when I'm away."

I was lucky at that initial stand with the Mills show . . . so much so that Mrs. Bernard Mills told me she was taking credit for having discovered me for them. I never will forget that it was she who got the attention of her husband off the horse acts long enough to make him notice me in New Haven, but I think that maybe Frank Wirth, the New York City circus booking agent, may have had a little something to do with it. Frank might have sent Bernard Mills and his wife to Connecticut that day to look at the Cole Brothers Circus and at the tramp clown.

During my first London engagement we'd hang out some evenings at a little hotel called Olivella's. Its basement reminded me of Sardi's Restaurant in New York because show people from many branches of the craft liked to congregate there after the show. There were pictures of the acts and the individual actors on the walls and the food was good. Bob Mathews and his wife and Bill Lawlor, the knife-thrower, went there with me. When I returned to England after the Second World War, I went to this hotel to see how it had come through. The front had been bombed out, but my old picture was still hanging on the wall inside.

There is in America a remarkable group called the Circus Fans Association. It was organized a quarter of a century ago by business and professional men and artists who at heart were still the small boys who wanted to run away with the circus. This group makes it a hobby to study and visit circuses and to help the shows with local problems when they come to town. They call the various chapters "tops," which is an expression for tents in America, and name them after circus people who either came from the community where the "top"

138

is or who are favorites of the Fans thereabouts. The Fans at Hagerstown, Maryland, honored me by naming their "top" for me a few years ago. The CFA has a fine magazine called *White Tops* for its membership. It was started by Karl K. Knecht, distinguished cartoonist of the Evansville, Indiana, *Courier-Journal,* and more recently edited by Walter Hohenadel.

But what I started out to say is that the British and the French have groups of Circus Fans, too, and they throw a big shindig at holiday time. Bernard Mills asked me if I would make an appearance at their New Year's party. So I took my broom and the props for my lumber gag, and I took along the easel and chalk-talk stuff just in case.

In a glittering ballroom filled with jewels and formal clothes and monocles galore suddenly appeared a hobo, trying to sweep the dance floor. It created a near sensation, for at first the guests thought I was a real bum who had wandered in off the street. Soon the women were hugging me and trying to dance with me and especially trying to make me talk. I nearly had to give up my silent character that night. A little later, I did the cartoon act, drawing a caricature of Bernard Mills, whose interesting features made him an easy subject, and one of Uncle Sam and of John Bull. The Mills brothers were surprised because they did not know I performed in this medium. It was three o'clock when I left and traffic was so thick it took an hour to move three or four blocks. It was 1938 and it had been a big year for a "bum."

When the Mills London Olympia engagement had run half its course, Cyril sent for me. I had no idea what he wanted, but despite the fact he had been courteous and pleasant to me I remembered that he had been far from convinced at the start that I could make an American hobo character a part of an English circus performance and I figured that

139

maybe he wanted me to change my routine. Instead, he asked me to go touring with them through the provinces the following summer.

This was a problem, for I had contracts to clown with indoor Shrine and Grotto Masonic Circuses during the rest of the winter in Detroit and Cleveland. I would have to go home and come back again to England if I were to tour with the Mills show. They worked it out and agreed to pay my boat fare back and forth, so I decided to do it. I had no formal contract with the Cole show in America for that next season.

I wanted to sail on the *Normandie,* which was a more expensive passage than my boat-fare contract with Mills provided, so I paid the difference and took the tug at Southampton. It was a day banked with fog, but just as we neared the giant liner, the fog lifted and there was that beautiful floating mountain looming over us. It was a sight I'll never forget.

I was paid off then and there for the difference in the fare. Remembering my seasickness of the other voyage, I had bought some popular seasick pills, but they did me no good. I still was sick for the first couple of days.

The winter indoor shows in America were then and still are put together for presentation under Masonic sponsorship so that money may be made for the wonderful hospitals which the Masons maintain for crippled children. The acts are booked either independently or in a package through such prominent circus people as Frank Wirth, Bob Morton, Orin Davenport or the Pollack outfit. They own no railroad cars, tents or wagons like a summer-touring circus. The program is more like vaudeville, but regularly in these winter dates the feature acts that have been with the tented show the previous summer appear.

In the Cleveland Auditorium that time, Clyde Beatty's act was one of the top attractions. To build up the psychological effect or showmanship of this act, somebody had dreamed up the idea of having twelve guards in uniform and with Springfield rifles march out into the arena while the announcer said: "Ladies and gentlemen, the guards are here for *your* protection during this highly dangerous and death-defying presentation. The trainer will protect himself."

The words hardly were out of the announcer's mouth when a big African male lion squeezed out of a break in the delivery chute and ran free in the hippodrome area. He was scared and jumped over a box where the mayor's wife, or some equally prominent person, was seated, and the lady fainted. The lion was corralled without injury to anyone, but the funny thing was that when the big cat first escaped, the "guards" dropped their rifles and ran in all directions. Some of them even climbed the aerial rigging.

Tonight has seen me assume the motley for the last time. It clung to my skin as I took it off, and the old cap and bells rang mournfully as I quitted them forever.

Joseph Grimaldi.
June 27, 1828

TENTING TONIGHT

I sailed back to England in a snowstorm aboard the *Queen Mary*. On my arrival in the London office of the Mills organization, Miss Moore said: "I have some bad news for you. The 'Governor' is down with pneumonia." This was Bertram Mills and it really was bad news to me because I liked him so much. I took a train to Luton on a cool, spring day, for this was the opening stand of the circus tour.

I could see the circus, set on a hill, for some distance before I reached the show grounds. It looked small as compared with the big American touring circuses, but it was a one-ringer after all and did not need to spread out as our big tops do. Two center poles sixty-five feet tall supported the sixteen-ounce canvas which was new each tour. At night, strings of electric lights were strung on the exterior of the tent, outlining it brilliantly and making it conspicuous for miles. The front or main entrance to the Mills show was built solid out of lumber instead of being merely a canvas marquee such as we have in this country. Overhead was the bandstand, under which the people walked to get into the circus proper.

From this vantage point the band could serenade the folks outside and act as a "come-on" as an American side-show band might do on the midway.

The colors of this circus are red and green and a portable green fence went all the way around the circus property, making its tents and wagons and other equipment a tight unity instead of a sprawl that went in all directions. They carry a baggage car filled with shrubs and vines and with these they trim the inside of the show where the people wander around between the main entrance and the seats. This area is the equivalent to our wild-animal menagerie tent, except that in the British circus it more resembles a theatre lobby with the greenery and the horses or some other animals, and a refreshment stand. When a circus moves only once a week, as these foreign shows do, it is possible to add these trimmings, but the American show moves every night and there is no time in the schedule for stringing lights outside to outline the shape of the main tent or for decorating with plants of one kind and another.

The Bertram Mills Circus had heavy grass carpet for the customers to tread once they were inside the big tent. There were box seats and the first eight rows of the chairs thereafter, on the incline, were covered with green velvet. The acts did not come in right out of the circus back yard or dressing-tent area; there was a sort of foyer where they lined up before coming through the entrance curtains into the main arena. The dressing tent for the clowns had a wooden floor in sections and a rug on it. The show carried cooking and dining facilities for the workingmen only; the rest of us were expected to take care of our own board and this we usually did in hotels or restaurants.

This circus moved on three railroad trains and leased its cars from the London, Midland & Scotland Railway in contrast to the way, in America, railroad shows own their rolling stock. Touring circuses in the States and in Canada pay freight rates on the basis of so much per car and so they have their flatcars, carrying the wagons, and stock cars carrying the horses, elephants and what is called "lead stock," as lengthy as possible. The British circus stock car has room for only a few horses and the flatcars carry only a couple of wagons per unit. They are about forty feet long instead of seventy as in the U.S.A. Seventeen stock cars were needed for the Mills horses, ponies, mules and elephants. The horse cars had built-in padded stalls so that the valuable stock was transported like race horses instead of loaded for space economy, which is the American system. What we call the boss groom or ringstock boss the British call the Master of the Horses; he comes from a coaching family, wears full dress with a flower in his lapel and is a prominent figure frequently invited to the best social functions in the cities where the circus plays. The man we call the circus boss canvasman is called, in England, the Tentmaster.

All told, fifty-seven railroad cars were needed to transport the huge Bertram Mills Circus that season. The smallest town we played was called March and we made it because the Mills family had promised to visit it on one of their tours. It really wasn't big enough for a regular engagement by a show the size of Mills, so we stayed only two days. In all towns, the lord mayor or his representative came the first night, made a speech of welcome and officially started the performance.

Three large motor vans traveled ahead of the circus into the towns where advertising and advance ticket selling was to be done. These carried cooking and sleeping accommodations for their crews as well as working and storage space. Our jumps were usually only forty or fifty miles between towns and the schedule was easy in other ways, too. Our matinees began at five o'clock and the evening performances at eight. On Sun-

145

days, church services were held in the main tent and townspeople as well as the show folks frequently attended.

Our performance ran two hours and about halfway through the announcer would say, "My lords and ladies, there will be a fifteen-minute interval." During this period, the property men would erect the steel arena for the wild-animal act which regularly started off the second half of the program.

I lived in small hotels and boardinghouses on that tour, but I cooked my own coffee in my room, as I never could get it to suit me otherwise. Food was plentiful then and it was inexpensive, so in spite of the fact that I did not have my board and sleeping quarters furnished by the circus, as in American circuses, the seventy-five dollars I was making per week went farther than the thirty-five I had been making with the Cole show.

For that first engagement under canvas, we rehearsed for a couple of days and were scheduled to open on Tuesday night. Bertram Mills died during rehearsals and his death dropped a curtain of sadness over the whole company. Many of the Mills employees had been with the old gentleman and his circus family for years and he seemed like a father to them. It had been his wish that the circus open as advertised whether he died or not, so we started off on that Tuesday night, then closed down the next day while services were held nearby at a town called Golders Green. This service in the chapel there was strictly formal. No circus band music was played; it was solemn throughout and the body was cremated.

To get back to the first Sunday I joined the outdoor troupe, I was saddled with my old feeling of loneliness and I wondered where everybody was. The pub opened at seven in the evening, and I was the only customer in the place. But five minutes later, the place was packed with my friends. They were nearly all there—the people who had been with the winter Olympia show and also one American, Bill Lawlor.

146

Soon I was playing darts with the Master of the Horses, a nice fellow named Tom Taggart, and my homesickness had vanished.

The Mills outfit has three separate tours and makes them successively over a period of three years. One is through the Midlands, including Wales. Another starts at Kent and plays the sea resorts in southern England. The tour we had started in 1938 goes up through the central part of England and north into Scotland.

Because the Mills show plays the same towns only once every three years, it need not change its program of acts as often as a show must do in the States where many of the same cities see the circus every year.

One thing I must set down about England is that television was in general use over there before we had it, and I was surprised to see the sets in the store windows. The Ringling Circus radio publicity department had used the clown Felix Adler on a television program in New York City as far back as 1932, but this was a novelty "one-shot" because television wasn't for public consumption in the States back then.

I did several radio shows in England and one television appearance as long ago as 1937. It was interview-style, of course, and I remember that the man who ran the broadcast kept asking me to tell him something funny that could be used as a tag or "pay-off" bit. I told him how once in Detroit, when some clowns had been taken to a hospital to entertain crippled children, we had been brought back to the show still dressed in our circus wardrobe and that I stopped in a small bank to cash a traveler's check. I was daydreaming and paying little attention to what I would look like to the bank clerk; I had been in there before, but always in street clothes. When they saw that hobo outfit, they must have thought I had come to stick up the bank the way they slammed the windows.

I found out what bad weather is on that tour, but it was

147

nothing to those Britishers. They expected it and the Scots came to the show rain or shine. It seldom poured down, that rain; instead it came in a fine mist that lasted all day. We had hot weather in August, but most of the time it was on the chilly side.

We were "tenting," as the British call their road tour, in Glasgow when Prime Minister Chamberlain went to Munich. The whole country was jumpy and circus business was way off. The people were staying home to listen to their radios. I was jumpy, too, for I had heard circus people tell about what a hell of a time they'd had in trying to get out of a country once war had been declared. I thought about the port city of Greenoch not far away and I remembered a wheelbarrow that we used to haul trunks. "I got first call on that wheelbarrow," I announced in the dressing tent. "If war is declared, I'm going to buy, borrow it or steal it and push my trunk the whole damn eighteen miles to Greenoch and hop a ship."

A guy in a Glasgow pub knew I was an American and gave me a hard time. "Why in hell doesn't Roosevelt do something?" he kept asking me. "Look," I'd reply, "I'm just a clown and this isn't my country and I'm not going to talk politics."

In the second week of our engagement there, I was clowning to half a house when Mr. Mills stopped the performance to make an announcement. He told the audience that the prime minister had reached an agreement with Hitler regarding Czechoslovakia and that there would be no war. A mighty cheer went up from the stands. The people didn't want war; they never do, but they have to fight them nevertheless and nobody realized in that happy crowd of circus spectators what was in store for them in the near future.

Business picked up and we played to packed tents. In York, I was called to the circus office wagon. Cyril and Bernard Mills were there and Cyril offered me a highball. "Kelly doesn't drink anything but beer," his brother told him. "Well, what about 1939, Mr. Kelly?" said Cyril Mills. "We like your work."

"I'd like to come back on two conditions," I told them. "One is that I get more money, and the other is that if we have another war scare like the one we just went through and it begins to look as if it will really happen, I want to be able to take off for home no matter where the circus is and without having you people feel that I ran out on you in the middle of a tour."

Both conditions were acceptable to the brothers. They put the money clause into the contract, and said it was the most they'd ever paid a clown during the tenting season. And on the "war" matter we simply shook hands.

The cathedral town of York was the closing stand and this was October. Bill Lawlor and I had a gin-rummy game going the whole tour and we kept books on it, but no money ever changed hands. Sometimes one of us would be into the other for five or six pounds, but when we totaled the tab on the train going into London we found that I owed him just ten shillings.

I had from October 30 until December 19, opening date of the Mills London Olympia show, "at liberty," but I couldn't take on any clowning for my labor permit did not allow me to work for anybody but Mills. This was all right with me. I wanted to do some sight-seeing, get some rest and make a trip to Paris.

I went back to the Kensington, but stayed only a few days. It was lonely without the circus crowd and I wanted to move nearer the center of town so I went to the Mount Royal at Marble Arch. A good many Americans stayed there and I liked to be able to buy American newspapers and magazines and cigarettes at the newsstand. The dining room was all right

149

and they made good American coffee. My room had facilities for electric cooking, so I set out to do some "batching" there. I hated to wash the dishes although I did it for several days until somebody tipped me off that dish washing was a hotel service and that the maid expected to do it. I bought things at Selfridge's and cooked for myself and enjoyed the rest from circus trouping. I went sight-seeing like any tourist, but I didn't do any romancing. I'd been dating a girl on the summer circus tour, but she wasn't in London now. A girl I had liked during the Olympia engagement the previous winter had put a chill on our friendship when she started working on me to take her back to the U.S.A.

Three weeks of just sitting around, doing nothing, was enough for me, so I arranged for a visa, went to Cook's and bought passage to France where Bob Mathews and his wife were working for a circus in Rouen. The Channel crossing was so rough and choppy that I knew I would be sick if I went inside. I tried to stay on deck all night where the air was fresh, even if cold, but eventually the waves commenced to splash me and the ship was bucking like a bronco in a rodeo. Inside, where I went now, everybody was sprawled out sick, but I managed to get to sleep before I became too nauseated and I woke up in the nice, quiet harbor of Dieppe.

Nobody could speak English except the travel agency, but from them I found out about the train to Rouen. I took a cab to the circus which was in a building surrounded by a kind of carnival with rides and shows and games covering all the space outside. I couldn't find anyone I knew, and nobody there spoke English, so I wandered away to a restaurant and there ran into Bob and Gertrude and an act I had known in the U.S.A. by the name of Kimri.

I had a lot of fun with these friends and I liked the circus performance in which a pair of clowns by the names of Mannetti and Ruhm were featured. They were talking clowns in

150

the old one-ring tradition and I did not understand anything they said, but I could get a pretty good idea from their pantomime. Mathews and his tightrope-walking lion, "Tuffy," were a feature of the circus, too.

A woman named Madame Loranti owned this show and she took us to her home for a party. It was quite an elegant affair, but there was nothing to eat except wafers which the people dunked in champagne. And they served none of my pleasure beverage, plain beer. At first, I thought that the wafers were appetizers, but they were the full and entire course of that party. At Mathews' suggestion, I had taken with me some pictures and other stuff that had been used about my clowning in the English papers. Madame Loranti was impressed and asked me to come to France and work in her circus when I had returned from the Mills tenting tour in 1939. I told her I would try to make it the next fall.

I went to the Hotel Carleton in Paris where my room looked over the famous cathedral of the Sacré-Coeur, a subject that artists like to paint. I had a hard time explaining to a taxi driver that I wanted to go to the Louvre. After listening to me stumble around in bum French for a while, he said: "Just where in the hell do you want to go?" That Frenchman took me for an interesting drive and talked to me about Paris all the way. I figured I was being taken for a sucker and that the cab fare would be higher than the Eiffel Tower, but it wasn't. He was just a nice guy who enjoyed making Paris attractive to strangers, and would have made a likely candidate for the diplomatic service.

The Louvre fascinated me. I loved the paintings and hardly could tear myself away. I went time after time, reflecting occasionally how startled people might be if I had come in my tramp makeup.

At night, we went to the Bal Tabarin, the Petit Casino and the Folies Bergère, and I particularly liked a place called

Tabac where showmen of all nations hung out. There was a
pool hall in the rear and a restaurant and bar in the front.
You'd run into plenty of show people there all right. Bill Lawlor introduced me to some French booking agents. I set up
my equipment and did the night-club act for them. One
wanted to send me to Milan and another to Latvia, and several of them said they would get me some work in Paris and
vicinity if I came back later for the French circus engagement.
At this time, I was seeing Lawlor and his wife off for Berlin.
The Mathewses had taken their lion to Stuttgart and that left
me a little on the lonely side. I took a boat back to London
and went to the Kensington to await the opening of the
Olympia.

During that engagement, I clowned for the Queen of
Spain, Haile Selassie, the Duke and Duchess of Gloucester
and Winston Churchill. The Spanish queen paid me no attention, and Selassie watched closely but did not applaud anything in the show. The Duke and Duchess had their children
along and the kids passed me a box of candy. I took the only
piece in the box that had a gold wrapper, for this candy I
meant to keep as a souvenir.

The clowns I dressed with told me one day that Churchill
was sitting in a box. "Who is Churchill?" I asked them. They
told me that he was a big politician and prominent in Parlia-
ment. He was sitting by himself, an unlit cigar in his mouth.
He looked relaxed and contented and he grinned when I did
the carpenter routine which now I had changed so that a sign
told people I was working for the ARP (Air Raid Precau-
tions) and was pretending to build a bomb shelter. I did my
act with little self-consciousness, scarcely dreaming events
would make one of my spectators one of the major figures in
history.

The Olympia had a King's Box for attendance by the
royal family, and I always took a quick look at it—way up
152

high—when I made my first entrance. Still, in the three times I played the building it never was occupied.

One night I was told that the head of the Ringling Brothers and Barnum & Bailey Circus, John Ringling North, was in the house. He came back to see me after the show, dressed in a conservative business suit, black Homburg and tightly rolled umbrella. He laughed when I started to talk, and said: "Here I thought you might be a foreigner and I wondered what language to use before I heard that Ozark drawl!"

Mr. North asked me how I liked it here and I told him I couldn't be happier if I had a million dollars. "Well, you'd just have to give most of it up to taxes anyhow," he said.

We did not talk business then, but he later asked a man named Strube to tell me that he'd like to have me work for the Ringling show when I returned to the States.

When I finished that engagement, I debated with myself about making a trip back to the States for the winter circus dates there and then having to return to England at my own expense. Another thing, I figured that once I got back to my country I might not want to return to England. If I breached that contract with Mills, I would have to pay the equivalent of one week's salary in sterling. At last my homesickness got the best of me and I decided to go home on the *Aquitania* with Strube and a troupe of girls who did aerial work on a lofty rigging, used mostly in buildings and on fair grounds because it was too tall for the tents, and the Cristiani family of bareback riders.

It was a rough winter crossing and the ship wasn't anything like the *Normandie* or the *Queen Mary* as far as accommodations were concerned. Lucio Cristiani was the comedian in the family riding act and he played the same role in the dining salon. The first morning at breakfast the ship was rolling and the chairs were emptying one by one. I had ordered, but said to Lucio that I felt I couldn't eat. He had a huge

153

breakfast before him and said to me, "It's a shame to leave all that good food." There was some other "comedy" about it and right in the middle of our conversation he jumped up from the table and took off like a shot. I didn't see him for two whole days and he looked a little pale when he did show up.

From New York, I went to play the indoor circus dates at Detroit, Rochester and Cleveland and then hurried home to see my folks. I had presents for them from London and we had a belated Christmas reunion. My boy, Emmett, Jr., was growing fast and his interests were developing in the direction of automobiles and mechanical matters—not in any kind of show business, and that was all right with his old man.

During the winter circus dates the performers had talked a lot about conditions abroad, and those who had bids for European appearances were wary of going over. I had recommended the Walter Guice high-bar act to Mills and had told him about an American clown named Paul Jung and his troupe of dwarfs. Mills and Guice didn't get together, but Jung was hired. At the last minute, he had to cancel because his wife went to the hospital.

I went back to England on the *Queen Mary* and hurried to the opening stand in Tombridge, Kent, with little time to spare. British trains are fine and they go like lightning, loading and unloading and streaking away as fast as the New York subways.

I showed up for the rehearsal period and the Mills brothers were pleased that on the radio program from the ship during my return to the States I had talked about their show. I had barely made that broadcast, for the old *Aquitania* was pitching like a leaf in the wind, and not until it was time for me to go on the program did I think I could stand up to it without becoming sick. On the show with me was Frank Bishop, engineer of the famous Royal Scot train that was going to America for exhibition at the World's Fair.

154

This time we toured the southern route. In our opening town there was an old ruined castle which I wanted to look over. Vines grew over it and there was a tower you could climb at your own risk. I went up and discovered that there was fresh lumber there and that an air-raid siren had been set. This didn't make me feel optimistic about the future of our tour. I had seen considerable "preparation" in troops drilling and artillery in practice while I was riding the train from London, and it looked too much like dress rehearsal to bode well.

We had a fine opening in good weather. I was listed on the show's advertising and the press agent, Stanley Williamson, did me a lot of favors. The Mills brothers told me I could stay with them as long as I wished, changing my gags when I felt like it, but continuing with the hobo character who had become popular with their audiences. All this made me feel good. If the threat of war hadn't been under the surface of all that grand "tenting," I would have been contented and relaxed as I had not been in years.

In Oxford, I noticed an impressive-looking man and an attractive woman with him in one of the boxes. In a hotel dining room, later, I saw them again and they introduced themselves. "I am Boswell, from South Africa," he said, "and we have a circus there." We knew a lot of the same people from circuses all over the world and we talked for hours until they threw us out of the place. He was getting ready to sail and wanted to buy sea lions. I told him about the place in Southern California. Boswell said if I would join him he would pay me for twelve months, even though his show didn't play that long a season. I thought about it as a date for the future, but of course the war came and blitzed that idea too.

The war news got worse and worse and so when our show played Brighton, little more than an hour from London by train, I went down there early. I told no one because I

155

didn't want to seem alarmist and, further, my gentlemen's agreement with Mills okayed my taking off at any point in the tour if it appeared war was imminent. I went to the U.S. Steamship Lines and asked a clerk how things looked. He told me, "All the Americans are heading for home."

The *President Roosevelt* was sailing Sunday and I tried to book passage. "I can't sell you a ticket," the clerk said. "We are even putting on three hundred cots, but they are all spoken for."

"When is the next ship?" I asked.

"The *Manhattan* is on its way here now from the States, and it is scheduled to sail back on September 3, but we aren't authorized to sell space on it yet because if war breaks out it may be turned back."

I offered this fellow a pound tip if he could get me on the ship, even if I had to sleep on the floor. I had come to England a "hobo" and I'd go home like one.

"I'll keep your request in mind," the man told me. "Come back at two o'clock when my boss is here."

From there I went to the American consul, told him about my agreement with Mills and that there was nothing to hold me. I asked his advice.

"My advice is to leave if you can," he said. "It looks bad and the news has looked worse since morning."

I said nothing about all this when I was back on the circus that evening, but asked Stanley Williamson what would happen to the show if war was declared. "We'd lose the train because we don't own it," he said. "The government would take it. And the news is bad. We guaranteed Poland and will go to war the minute Hitler moves."

Frank Foster told me the same thing. "I think I will take my trunk into London on Saturday night and store it so it

156

won't be on the show if anything happens fast," I said to Foster. There was no train on Sunday; the last one left for London at 10:20 Saturday night.

I knew I had to catch that train. I had done a good deal of soul searching about my going home at this time and I finally reached the conclusion that a clean break would be better for all concerned. I would explain in a letter to Mills my reasons for wanting to be in my own country in the event of war—as a matter of fact we had reached agreement on this point at the time I signed the contract.

In London, I was afraid I would miss the boat train, so I took a room in a hotel across from Waterloo Station. The boat train left late and was jammed with soldiers everywhere. At the pier everybody was herded into a big room which was hot as blazes. The steamship people were off schedule because of having to set up the cots, etc., for extra passengers, so we waited four hours. During this time I had seen my trunk going aboard. A circus trunk is easily located because it looks like nothing else in the world. I don't mean it is painted in loud colors or that it has an odd shape; it just stands out somehow.

When I went aboard, the ship looked like a New York commercial hotel during a national convention. There were cots in every public room except the dining rooms and the bars. The halls had them too, each with linen and a blanket on top and a life preserver underneath. I immediately rented a deck chair, a cushion and a blanket. This was to be my bed in case I didn't get a cot. The purser, who turned out to be an ex-burlesque comedian, knew me by name and tried to get me a berth. But he had one less space than he'd figured. When I went to the cabin, it was filled and the men in there were staying in their berths so nothing would happen to make them lose out.

On the way back, I got lost and wandered into a port-

157

able-curtain "dormitory" loaded with women in various stages of undress. They squealed and I got red in the face and hurried on out of there. I then left my suitcase at the end of a hallway while I tried the purser again. When he had assigned me to a cot, I couldn't find the suitcase. I spent an hour looking for it and was giving it up for lost when I stumbled over it. I had been looking in the wrong hallway. It was right where I had left it and I was relieved—seeing as how everything else I owned was in the trunk and the trunk was somewhere deep in the hold of the ship.

When I was lucky enough to get a cot, I felt it was the best bed I ever had. When we left England, I looked back at the buildings of Southampton and thought to myself how those slate roofs would be flying through the air from German bombs if war came. I knew that if I had guessed wrong, I would be out of a job for the rest of the summer and that I would look frightened and foolish to the Mills people. I would have run away for nothing and that would be exactly what my standing with them would be good for—nothing. Many who wanted passage so much they would have slept on deck were left behind because the officials protested that we were overloaded already. We had three hundred over capacity and the ship had lifeboats for only six hundred; there were rafts for the remainder.

Postmaster Jim Farley was aboard with his two daughters. At the ship movies that night somebody dared me to ask him for a postage stamp. I leaned over and told him I had a letter to mail and needed a stamp. He laughed and said, "I'm sorry, but I'm not carrying any tonight."

I slept late and found the ship's newspaper on my cot every morning. But the day war was declared, the steward woke me up. I knew what he was going to say. "Hitler moved into Poland at daybreak. England declared war at eleven o'clock."

I was glad to be on my way home, but my thoughts went back to England. During the stop in Ireland, I had sent Bernard and Cyril Mills a letter to explain my departure. I heard from them later. They said in their letter that it was perfectly all right for me to leave, for we had agreed upon it beforehand. Lawlor was sore at me for not telling him I was going to leave, but he got over it later on when he found out how difficult it was to get out of England once war had started. He and his wife got a ship after some weeks of no work. Bob Mathews and his wife went broke in Belgium before they got out. Their lion had to follow them in another ship; they were lucky to get him out at all. Con Colleano, the tightwire star, was playing in Germany when the war broke. He is Australian-born and a British subject although his home is in New York. He had seen the war coming and with his wife, Winnie, had laid careful plans for jumping into Switzerland. They made it all right, but by so narrow a margin that Con had to "blow" his rigging. (In outdoor show business to "blow" something is to lose it or have to leave it behind.)

When I heard all this, I felt sorry for the show. It all happened just as Foster and Williamson had predicted. The government requisitioned the railroad cars at once and the show closed. Most of the equipment was stored in London; the horses were shipped north.

News reached us that a Cunard passenger liner had been sunk. This ship had sailed from Greenoch Harbor, and I might have been on it if it had been one year sooner and I'd made good my threat to wheel my trunk all the way to Greenoch to get out of the country.

I listened to a radio speech by the King and I watched the news bulletins which became worse by the hour. That

159

night, we flew the Stars and Stripes all night, with two spotlights trained on the flag, to avoid being sunk by a German submarine. Lashed to the deck at the prow of our ship was a model British PT boat and there were several English officers with it. It was covered with canvas, but the nose stuck out and anyone could see what it was. Nobody was allowed in it. It was being sent to America to be put into production. I heard that the captain said he'd feel more comfortable when the thing was off his ship.

Soon we were off the Grand Banks of Newfoundland and that night we saw a great many twinkling lights. A lot of us passengers worried about that, but the captain explained: "Those are fishing craft off Newfoundland. Ordinarily you'd not see them, but I am going a little north of my regular course on this trip and that's why you see them. In case of our ship taking a torpedo, we probably could get in and receive rescue help from the small boats."

When I heard that, I decided that this was the night to sleep in my deck chair. It was a fine night and I slept until almost noon. On that day I was asked to take part in a ship show. I didn't think they could find my trunk, but somehow they did and I put on my tramp outfit. Kids followed me all over the ship until I felt like the Pied Piper.

I had been down in the baggage room, locating my trunk, when I'd smelled something wonderful. Piled to the ceiling in greased paper with metal bands around the bales was pressed tobacco that had been shipped to England for processing and now was on its way back to the States to be packed. Tons of copper to have been dropped at Hamburg was still on the ship because we had not touched that port.

Ambrose Light and the twinkling gems of Coney Island were a sight to see, but the real thrill came in the morning. I have seen some beautiful women in more than thirty years of trouping, but nothing to touch the Lady who met us in the

New York harbor. It made my eyes fill with tears to see her standing there, the torch of liberty lifted in her hand.

I was plumb fortunate. I had taken a chance in going back to England the winter before. It was strictly crowding my luck. But somehow I had managed to "touch all the bases" and I was safe at home.

> Let . . . clowns speak no more
> than is set down for them.
>
> *Hamlet*

STAGE DOORS

When I got off the boat, I checked into the old Cadillac Hotel and headed straight for the World's Fair. I had expected to miss it entirely, on account of the European trip, but now I was back in time to see it.

It was an amazing show and I enjoyed it, but I found myself hanging around the British and the Irish exhibits most of the time, and wondering about my friends with the Bertram Mills Circus. I couldn't shake it off. My mind was still with the people whose country had gone to war.

The Ringling show was out on the West coast and Cole Brothers Circus was somewhere in the Midwest and it was late to be joining a circus anyhow, so I decided to take a crack at Broadway. Olsen and Johnson's *Hellzapoppin* was at the Winter Garden and a smash hit. I went to watch it and came away with an idea. Next day I went to see the two comedians and had a chat with them. They told me how lucky I was to get out of Europe, but I kept turning back the conversation to how I was out of work and needed a job—and that maybe my kind of clowning might fit into that wild scramble at the Win-

163

ter Garden. The show took place on the stage, in the aisles, in the lobby and all over the house. "Wonderful," they said. "Try it and see how it fits in."

Well, nobody could say more than that. I figured I was just one gag removed from a Broadway reputation. Next evening I went into the show. I worked the carpenter routine in the aisle before the curtain rang up. First, I walked out onto the stage apron and threw a board onto the floor. I had rusty nails in it which made a horrible squeak when I tried to pull them. I then carried the board down into the aisle and stuck it almost in some poor customer's face and started to drive nails in it. This was strictly off-beat for the start of a musical show, but so was everything else in *Hellzapoppin*. They even had a guy prance down the aisle from the back of the house and sing a ballad before the curtain went up. During intermission, I was still working on my "project" in the foyer and at the end of the show the customers found me out in the street, trying to nail my lumber up on the marquee. It amused them so much that they jammed up there till a cop made me stop so he could clear the sidewalk.

I went back to the hotel, satisfied that I was a hit. I had stopped traffic on Broadway.

But not for long. Next day, when I saw Olsen and Johnson, they told me I must go and make a deal with the Shuberts if I wanted to work in the show. I went, and was told that the show was a sellout with or without my clowning and that the salary I was asking them was too high. They did say something that encouraged me, however. "Come back and see us next spring. We are going to do a show that your kind of tramp comic might fit like a glove."

That was the end of my Broadway smash. I had "opened and closed in one," as they say in the theatre.

The next day, the country boy took his mind off Broadway and wired a booking agent in Detroit. He booked me into a night club in Louisville. It was to be a one-week stand and the club was some distance out of the city. I took a room in a nearby tourist camp and had all day to look around. The countryside was beautiful. Grapes were in season. I had seen none in England and I spent the afternoon nibbling at the fruit as I wandered in the fields. I was a farm boy again, home from abroad, and glad to be.

Later, I set up my easel and got the rest of my props ready and waited around the night club. It was deserted except for the bartender, so I sat at the bar and ordered a beer.

In came a guy with a bag of silver and started filling the cash register. I reckoned he must be the manager. He gave me a long, straight look and asked if I was one of his entertainers. I told him I did a novelty act. "Well, I am not going to have any boozers on my show *this* week," he said with his jaw stuck out and his fist clenched.

"I don't figure I'm 'boozing,' " I told him. "I am sitting here having a beer."

"Every single man I have had this season has been a lush!" he complained. "I had to fire the master of ceremonies last week because he was drunk for the first four shows!"

I thought this one over and finally said: "Listen, Mister. I drink beer, but I don't get drunk and I never have missed a performance in my life. And I don't care if I open here or not. I am a circus clown by trade and I am always on deck when it is time for me to go on."

He said nothing more, but turned away with a disgusted look on his face as if to say, "Just another guzzler."

After the first show, I heard somebody knocking on my door. It was this same fellow. "You've got a good act," he said. "I want you to draw a picture of that guy sitting at the ringside table, and then give it to him; he's an important customer."

I did it and the customer was pleased and the manager

165

was more so. From then on, he was my pal, and I never had to buy another beer.

Later, when I opened one spring with the Cole show, which wintered in Louisville and usually made that city its first stand, my night-club friend was the first person to come back to the dressing tent and shake my hand. "Listen," he said, "I had you figured wrong. I've been a saloon keeper most of my life. I sell it and I don't drink it and I'm prejudiced, but I've seen it louse up some pretty talented people."

After that night-club date in Kentucky, I went to a place called the Log Cabin, north of Toledo. It was a pleasant engagement, but I ate something that hit me wrong and fainted after my first show. They found me on the dressing-room floor. I had been talking with some jugglers on the bill and just passed out. A doctor came and gave me some sort of shot and later I did the second show with no ill effects.

My Detroit booker kept me working until time to fill some winter circus engagements, and when I was working in Philadelphia I got the letter I had been waiting for years. It was from Pat Valdo of the Ringling Brothers and Barnum & Bailey Circus—"Big Bertha," the "Big One," "The Greatest Show on Earth."

I wanted it mightily, but I still had in mind the thing that the Shubert theatrical office had talked about—a good part in a Broadway show. I went in from Philadelphia with Harold Voise and his wife, who were aerialists in the winter circus engagement we had just finished. I went to the Shubert office, figuring it was just a long shot, but something I should follow up. They almost kissed me. "Where the hell have you been? We've been looking all over for you!" they said.

The show was *Keep Off the Grass,* a musical set in Central Park in the early days of Old New York, and the stars were to be Ray Bolger, Jimmie Durante and Jane Froman— pretty fast company for the kid from Kansas.

"What about money and a contract?" I wanted to know.

"We'll give you a term contract with an option to open; after that, you'll get a run-of-the-play contract, which is for the life of the play."

It sounded all right to me and the money was okay, too. When I told Harold Voise about it, he was tickled to death. "This may be a big thing for you, Emmett," he said. "When you go back to circus clowning, you'll have a Broadway address in your kip and you will command more respect and get more money."

I passed up the Ringling offer, but I did it reluctantly. I always had wanted to troupe with the "Big One" and I wasn't sure they would ask me again if I turned down the first offer.

There was some time before rehearsals began for *Keep Off the Grass,* so in those weeks I went to Indiana to see my folks. It was a fine reunion. I returned to New York City and checked into the Hotel Belvedere in time for the beginning of rehearsals at the Golden Theatre. In this four-week period before we tried out the show in Boston, prior to New York's premiere, I received rehearsal pay and had to join Actors Equity, the actors' union.

I attended the endless rehearsals, sat and waited to be asked to do something and never was called on stage. Eddie Dowling was in charge of the sketches. He said to me, "Don't worry, just sit tight. We'll have something for you."

Finally they handed me two songs. One was called "On the Old Park Bench" and the other was "Cabby's Serenade." I told them that I worked in pantomime and couldn't sing anyhow. "Okay, you just work your mouth and fake it," they told me. Jackie Gleason, Sid Walker, Peanuts Bohn, Larry Adler and Hal Neiman and I were cast as hack drivers. There was a tree surgeon scene that Durante worked. He objected to my going into it in my tramp clown makeup.

167

"They'll all be watching him," Durante said. "He should work 'straight' without that hobo makeup."

I objected to that, so they left me out of that scene. Then I had an idea. I suggested: "Why don't you just forget me as far as the show is concerned, and let me free-lance. I'll be a street cleaner, I'll get a push cart and a broom, white coat, and I'll work on the stage apron before the curtain goes up. I'll work as though I have no idea there is anyone in the theatre and for a clincher I'll dump the swept-up popcorn on the orchestra leader's head."

This did not register very well with the powers that be. "They will say we are stealing Olsen and Johnson's stuff," they argued. "And the orchestra leader won't be the happiest man on earth, either."

So I wound up in the "Cabby's Serenade" after all. Six of us "bums" came in—three from each side—and I mugged it. Peanuts Bohn gave me some advice: "Don't try to sing; just do your pantomime and you'll steal the scene."

I gave it all I could and when we were supposed to sing "The Horse with the Hansom Behind," I got quite a few laughs, just being my sad self. Jimmy McHugh raised the roof about this. "We spend six thousand dollars for a song that people can't hear because they are laughing at you!"

The next number was a Latin thing that I did not like, but managed to get through somehow. Then came the trip through the museum. I was cast as one of the spectators who had wandered into the place by mistake. I had a straw hat in my hand and as a last-minute idea I pushed up my hair, and for some reason it got a laugh. Jimmy worried about this laugh, too, because it wasn't supposed to be there.

In my next appearance, I was asleep on a park bench and Larry Adler's harmonica woke me up. I had my lunch in a paper sack and proceeded to eat it. What got the laugh was my using a toothbrush afterward. I don't know what

168

made it funny. In the circus, we try to do off-beat bits and build a laugh on the unexpected. I figured the stage would be the same way.

We got fair notices in Boston and took the show to New York. I was lonely because the Ringling show had just left Madison Square Garden and with it were a lot of my circus pals I had wanted to see. The show got only so-so reviews in the big town, but one day Ray Bolger came to my dressing room and said, "Have you seen *Time Magazine?*"

I hadn't, but I went out and bought one and it contained the one and only legitimate theatre notice I ever received, and it was pretty good for a country boy. It read, ". . . and there's a bum, Emmett Kelly, who would leisurely proceed to eat a ham sandwich out of a paper poke while a bunch of other bums sang a park bench song; then he would lazily brush his teeth with the dry stub of a toothbrush, which provides the one inspired moment of an otherwise uninspired show." It was rough on the show, for there were good things in it and wonderful people to work with. It ran a while, but cannot be listed in the book as a big hit.

Back home again to Indiana went the farm boy. I hooked up some night-club dates for the balance of the season, and in this string I played the Alpine Village in Cleveland, Ohio. It always has been my favorite stand in that field of entertainment. One year I made it twice and in all I have played it eight or nine times. It is an old-fashioned, beer-garden kind of family place and run by nice folks. There wasn't any trouble with drunks in that place, although they had bothered me in some other clubs—making cracks and trying to crack up the act. I learned that if I drew a caricature of the troublemaker, it usually would flatter him and make him shut up, and of course it amused the other customers who were also glad to have the bore put in his place.

I made another visit to Indiana and then played the win-

169

ter circus dates and got sweet on a girl in one of the acts. The Ringling show made me an offer, but I didn't want to start there at the kind of salary they first offered. Valdo said he couldn't pay me any more, so I went to work for Zack Terrell, owner of Cole Brothers Circus, for the money I couldn't get from the "Big One."

Another reason I took the Cole job was that that circus was willing to place the girl I was going with. Terrell said he would give her a job and break her into the aerial production numbers and see how she made out. Then one day, while I was still playing the winter dates and the circus was busy getting ready for the road, he telephoned me from winter quarters in Louisville. He had just fired his painter and wanted me to come on and finish lettering the cages and the ticket wagons. I was busy with the brush when my girl saw me there for the first time. There was paint smeared on me and I didn't add up to her idea of a big-time circus performer. The upshot was that she gave me the cold shoulder, and we never did warm up to each other after that.

The circus paint and the animals and the fresh canvas smelled wonderful to me. I knew then that, great as it was, the theatre never would mean to me what the circus did. The tent that year was something to behold. The canvas in the center sections of the big top was made with stripes and stars in a field of blue. Cole Brothers Circus had two of these tents made like that especially for the war years and used them until they wore out.

Jack Dempsey joined the circus for the last seven weeks of its tour and a special railroad car was provided for him. He was a lot of fun and proved to be quite an attraction, although his performance was merely to referee the wrestling match in the aftershow or "concert." Jack was a great practical joker. He liked to put a match in somebody's shoe when the victim wasn't looking and light it. When the match burned

170

down to the shoe, it would heat the foot harmlessly and give the owner the "hot foot." Jack had a buzzer palmed in his big hand and when he shook hands with somebody, the thing would surprise the other fellow plenty. Dempsey's wife and daughters came to visit for a few weeks and they were all good company.

We were playing in the Deep South toward the end of that tour when Pat Valdo and John Ringling North came to visit us. The Ringling show was playing nearby. I remember that Johnny North was wearing a riding habit. He likes horses and rides well. There was no opportunity for conversation with these distinguished guests, but Valdo managed to whisper to me, "Write me a line right away about next year!"

That meant that the Ringling personnel director had seen me for the third time and that John North had, too, and that they still liked my work. It encouraged me, so I wrote a letter next day and pretty soon had a reply. In spite of the fact that I was working for more money than the Ringling show had been willing to give me a year ago, I asked for more and my offer was accepted. They sent me a contract general delivery which I opened in the post office in the presence of my pal, Harold Voise. He was as pleased as I was. "This is it, Emmett," he said. "You're going to work for 'Big Bertha.' "

The Cole Brothers Circus expected me to come back the following season and when I told Mr. Terrell that I had a Ringling contract, he wasn't exactly pleased. "This is your home, Emmett," he argued. "You've been happy here. How much did they offer you?" I wouldn't reveal the salary, but he said, "Whatever it is, I'll top it."

This was flattering, but I figured that the time had come to move up and I told him so. He was fine about it and wished me luck.

Everything looked rosy now, except for the fact that a man named Hitler was giving the world plenty of trouble. I was playing a night-club date in Cincinnati, and on a Sunday afternoon, December 7, I had my little portable radio turned on. I almost cut my throat with my razor when I heard the news that the Japs had bombed our fleet in Pearl Harbor. I ran down the hall where a dance team was living and they had heard it, too. A lot of things raced through my mind. How many ships had they caught in that bombing? How many lives lost? What about my eighteen-year-old boy now that we were in the war? What about the circus?

I can remember only one other day that affected me so strongly—the day I got news that my mother had died. That was almost exactly nine years later. I was at the window of my room in the Hotel Roosevelt watching through binoculars the Christmas Lane Parade on Hollywood Boulevard. The telephone rang. It was my niece calling from Lafayette, Indiana, to tell me my mother was gone. I hadn't spent much time with my mother in recent years, but just knowing she was in the same world with me always lifted my spirits. Being blessed with a mother like mine would give anybody a lot to be thankful for. And I was certainly thankful for her that Pearl Harbor Day.

I went to a naval recruiting station the next morning and quickly learned that they did not want any forty-two-year-old guys without previous service experience. My son was eligible, but his old man wasn't. Emmett Leo Kelly, Jr., enlisted in the Navy. His pappy would return to the circus and keep on being a hobo clown—if there *was* any circus.

I wrote to Pat Valdo and he replied that as near as he could tell the big show would roll as usual. At least I had a job.

But I thought about my circus friends in England and how they had closed up the Bertram Mills show in a hurry as soon as the war began. I wondered how long "Big Bertha" would last if bombs started falling over here.

The news, however, was good for the moment. In the circus business there is today's town and tomorrow's town and we always look ahead. I had my first contract with the biggest circus in the world and it seemed like a long way for the kid from Kansas to have come. I felt pretty good in spite of everything, so I went out and bought my first war bond and a ticket for New York City to join "The Greatest Show on Earth."

The calli-ope is screaming and bright flags are riding high
On circus canvas billowing like clouds against the sky;
Lions, tigers, painted clowns and elephants troop past,
And bands play spangled music, for it's circus day at last.

THE BIG TIME

You can troupe all over the world, and you can listen to applause in far-away places and you can read flattering publicity from hell to breakfast, but when you open with Ringling Brothers and Barnum & Bailey in Madison Square Garden, New York City, you have "arrived."

The "Big One" comes straight from its winter quarters in Florida where it has been preening itself during the four months of the non-touring or "off" season. It is newly painted from stem to stern and its quarter-million-dollar wardrobe is a sight to behold.

On its own railroad train it streaks up out of Dixie, making two stops en route for feeding and watering the animals, and it unloads in the Mott Haven Yards—some miles uptown from the Garden, which is at Eighth Avenue between 49th and 50th Streets and almost in the center of town.

The haul from the railroad yards to the building takes place at night when the traffic eases off. The streets of the big city echo to the unfamiliar clop-clop of hundreds of hoofs and if it is quiet enough, people can hear the soft scraping swosh-swosh of the elephant march. The big red wagons roll downtown and the whole caboodle is put into the building— animals in the basement, where they are exhibited along with the side-show attractions; props and rigging in the big arena on ground level. Dressing rooms are on three levels and just about all over the place. A hundred truckloads of dirt have been brought in and spread on the concrete floor. This dirt is valuable and is hauled away and saved from year to year. Maybe the Garden uses the same dirt for the annual horse show and the rodeo—I don't know. But I know that overnight the Garden people can turn the arena from an ice-hockey rink into a circus hippodrome. It is fast, efficient work that circus people, always fighting time and space, appreciate.

Sometimes there are only a couple of days for rehearsals in the Garden, but most of the show has been in practice at winter quarters anyhow and Pat Valdo is a past master at putting a circus performance together. He and the band leader and the boss property man, the chief electrician and the equestrian director go to work on it and fit the various units into a fast-moving crazy quilt of entertainment.

The morning after the show moves in, the performers all gather in street clothes on the arena floor, mill around and say hello to friends they haven't seen for a long time; meet the new foreign acts and get their positions for "spec," which is circus slang for the spectacle or the major production number. It is like a parade and it is always lavish in the extreme. Usually it has a theme such as "Old King Cole and Mother Goose," "Marco Polo," "Cinderella," "Alice in Wonderland," etc.

The "spec" the year I joined the show was "American Holidays" with floats and other parade units representing the days we celebrate in this country. I ran into a lot of old acquaintances that first day in the Garden—clowns and acrobats and animal trainers and aerialists, including Arthur

Willie on Broadway: the "Cabbies' Serenade" in *Keep Off The Grass*.

The "Old Park Bench" in *Keep Off The Grass* (*Left to right:* Larry Adler, Hal Neiman, Sid Walker, Jackie Gleason, Peanuts Bohn, Emmett Kelly).

(*Photos by Fred Fehl*)

(H. A. Atwell Studi

Frustration and despair
are Willie's most fre-
quent moods.

Willie and his favorite newspaper.

Lucky at cards . . . .

. . . . unlucky at love.

Sometimes children don't know what to make of Willie.

(*Ringling Bros. and Barnum & Bailey*)

Willie has a musical soul too.

Hunting big game under the big top.

(Burnell, Sarasota, Florida)

Keeping in practice on a backyard trapeze in Sarasota.

Always the sportsman, Willie catches his dinner.

(*Lawrence D. Thornton, New York*)

Easy does it, Willie!

Emmett into Willie.

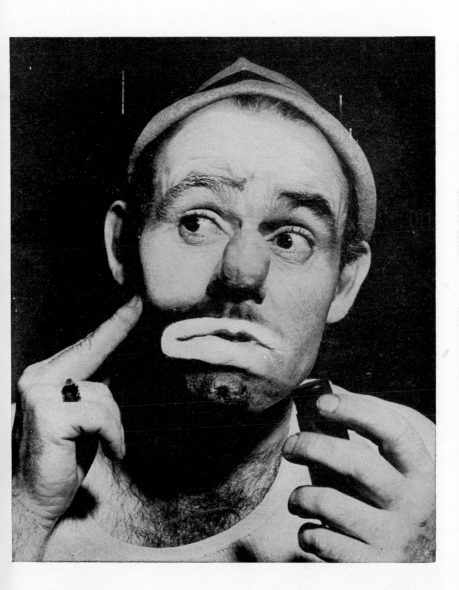

Willie has never got the farm out of his blood.

Willie is off to join "Ike."

(Rolland W. Lee, L

Emmett Kelly

Concello who had been one of the best flying-trapeze leapers and who now was manager of the circus for Johnny North, the president. Concello is young looking and has a light complexion and is built like most of the aerialists—medium height or slightly less, slim legs, big shoulders and muscular arms. The only tall, slim guy I ever knew who made the big-time in the air is Albert Powell. And his act was aerial contortion rather than straight single trap or flying-return. He used the momentum of his body to make up for what he lacked in arm muscle. The short, heavy arm muscles are better to have in this work than the long muscles.

The Ringling general manager had trained a lot of fliers and he kept a regular winter school in the old Eddie Ward training quarters at Bloomington, Illinois. His pride and joy was his wife, Antoinette, who was poetry in the air and a feature of the "Big One" for several seasons. She can still fly with the best, but since their boy Randy came, she devotes most of her time to teaching aerial work to the up-and-coming youngsters with the circus.

I was feeling pretty cocky at having made the "big-time" at last when something happened that changed the complexion of things. The wardrobe boss said, "Kelly, you better go downstairs and try on your costumes."

My costumes? I had only one costume—the hobo outfit. What were they trying to do to me?

I went to the wardrobe department and found that they had me set into three production numbers in addition to my individual clowning. One number was a thing called "The Wedding of Gargantua and Toto." The circus had just bought a female gorilla to exhibit alongside the giant-size gorilla Gargantua (although they never were mated) and was making a lot over it—even to a burlesque wedding parade. For this one, I was cast as a jailer on the outside of a gorilla cage. In "spec" I was to ride a float in some fantastic costume, and for a third

193

production number I was to be a web-sitter, which is the circus name for an aerialist's assistant or ground-man.

This was bad news to me. If I had to keep changing costumes throughout the performance, I would not have time to make enough appearances in my regular hobo wardrobe. I knew that I must come out again and again in the same outfit so I could make an impression on the public. It couldn't be just now and then; it had to make its point by repetition. I would do different clown routines at each appearance, but I would always look the same.

I felt so low that I wandered out of the building and went across the street to a saloon and sat with a beer. It tasted flat—like my future with the "Big One." I hardly knew what to do. But one thing I was sure of: I wouldn't go back on "Willie," my tramp-clown character. If they tried to lose "Willie," they'd lose me too. I considered shooting a wire to the Cole show, but gave that up because I really didn't want to go crawling back there and maybe have to take less money to boot.

A little later, I told Valdo about my problem. "You'll have to work it out with John Murray Anderson," he told me. "He's in charge of the production numbers."

Now I knew that this John Murray Anderson, a prominent Broadway theatrical name recently engaged to do some circus work, was born a Britisher. So I gathered up some of my London reviews and general publicity from the British Isles and collared him after rehearsal in the wardrobe room.

Anderson was a very busy man. That day he looked older than his middle years and there were tired lines under his gray hair. His shoulders sagged and his expressive hands worked slowly as he handled some of the new wardrobe and showed the women how he wanted the extravagant clothing to "hang" on the wearers. "Mister Anderson," I said, "I have been with the Bertram Mills Circus in England and I have

194

been wanting to show you these things so you will know how I had planned to work in the Ringling performance."

He looked over my clippings and said, "These are jolly good all right—very interesting. What do you propose to do?"

That gave me the opening. I explained about the importance of continuity in a character like mine and I begged him to excuse me from the production numbers for just the dress rehearsal so I could give him a "showcase." I knew there would be some guests at the dress rehearsal—enough so that I could maybe make an impression and prove my point with Anderson. He said to try it that way.

I got into my rags and grabbed the broom for my first appearance, which was to be the business of trying to sweep the spotlight out of the arena. I looked in the mirror at "Willie." I had a heart-to-heart talk with him that night. "Now, 'Willie,' " I said silently, "this is the 'BIG One.' This is where we started for a long time ago. We made this one the hard way. There's white-tie-and-tails out there tonight in those boxes and this is the Garden and the biggest city in the world and 'The Greatest Show on Earth.' "

"Willie" wasn't impressed, as I remember it. "Look, you hayseed," he cracked back at me. "I was doing all right back on that old drawing board in Kansas City. But you had to take me off and make a gypsy out of me. If I let you down tonight, there's only one fellow I know we could throw the blame on. And he looks a lot like you!"

I did the broom routine and got a smattering of applause —no indication of how I might be going over. The show hadn't begun yet. My first appearance was a preliminary. I had gone over the running order of the acts and had figured where I would fit in. Now I stood waiting for the performance to begin. I peeked through a crack in the big, wide, swinging entrance doors. Merle Evans had his baton lifted, and Fred Bradna, dressed in riding habit with red coat and black silk hat, had his whistle in his mouth. He blew one short blast and Evans' baton came down. Fanfare! Then the announcer's voice booming out: "Children of all ages— Ringling Brothers and Barnum & Bailey presents the 1942 edition of 'The Greatest Show on Earth!' "

From then on I was working in a field of lightning. It was the fastest-moving thing I ever saw. I had to be careful to work my special kind of clowning into the arena when it would not conflict with the principal turns, and I had to be mighty careful about "stealing" attention from them. But I kept working as usual and about halfway through the performance, Mr. Anderson sidled up to me and said: "Mister Kelly, I have been watching you and I like the way you work. You are an artist and you can forget change of costume and the production numbers that we had scheduled you to appear in. Just carry on."

Well, I can tell you that the world lifted off poor "Willie's" shoulders at that moment and for the rest of that dress rehearsal he floated on a pink cloud. When it was over, I went back to that saloon where I had sat so dejected a few hours before and *that* beer I really enjoyed. I was happy and relaxed. I wasn't going to have to leave "Willie" in the dressing room while I changed to other costumes and went into other numbers that would be meaningless to my clown part. These people were professionals and they realized what I was trying to do. This was really the "Big One," and now it was my home.

Everybody made me welcome. My neighbors in "clown alley" were Paul Jung and Dutch Lully, Paul Jerome, Jack LeClair, Felix Adler, Lou Jacobs and Willie Mosier. Willie doubled as circus mailman and as the locksmith for the show. He had hundreds of trunk keys and if a performer lost his key, Mosier always could find one that would open the trunk.

196

He was as tall as an Indiana basketball player and one of the funniest clown gags in the show was the bit where Mosier stood on the track with his legs spread and his little pet donkey walked between them and scooped up his master and took him away on his back.

Valdo had said to me: "Now, Emmett, I know I don't have to say this to an old trouper, for you have been around, but you are new here and your work is different from anything we ever had with the show. We never before now permitted a clown to 'free-lance' and work throughout the show more or less on his own. You do it well and you will get publicity. Don't show it in the dressing room or try to become a star inside of four days."

And Valdo cautioned me about a couple of other things. He told me not to work while the Cristiani bareback-riding act was on or while Truzzi, the juggler, was working.

I was a "First-of-May" again, at least as far as the "Big One" was concerned and I knew it and watched my step. I did get a lot of publicity because I was a novelty in this show. The papers and radio stations seemed to forget that a few years before this I had been in town at the Hippodrome with the Cole show and had done much the same kind of clowning. They treated me like a brand new kind of circus comic.

The circus is a small world with so many obstacles to buck every day that we ordinarily lose track of what is going on outside. But this was the first year of the war and I had encouraged my elder son to enlist in the Navy, so I was busy reading the news every day. Emmett, Jr., did some trouping too. He went from Great Lakes Naval Training to Norfolk, to New Orleans, to Fort Lauderdale, to San Francisco, and finally aboard an LST (#365) where he saw quite a bit of action, including some of the show at Okinawa. I checked my draft status from time to time and decided that if they got around to fellows my age, I would try for the Navy, too. Then at least my boy and I would be in the same business for a while.

One of the interesting dates the Ringling circus keeps every year in New York is with Bellevue Hospital where we go with a one-hour, makeshift performance that is presented in the outside courtyard for the patients there. This is a morning show and always is scheduled in late April, toward the end of our Garden engagement, so we will have a good chance at pleasant weather. I played my first Bellevue show that time in 1942 and was surprised that the circus had been going there for more than half a century—clear back to the Barnum & Bailey days before there was any Ringling-Barnum combination of titles.

After the Madison Square Garden engagement of from four to six weeks, the big show moves to Boston and plays indoors at Boston Garden for a week or ten days. While this is going on, the rest of the circus equipment—tents, wagons, etc., leaves Sarasota on two trains and is set up in whatever city is to be the opening stand under canvas. The new tents are put in the air and the canvas city laid out just as it will be in one hundred fifty towns big and small as the show moves over the map.

In 1942, the opening stand was Baltimore and when I saw that spread of fresh canvas I got a whale of a thrill. It was big and it was beautiful.

It is always a kick to see how performers from foreign countries react to the size of the "Big One." I remember that in my first season on the Ringling show, there was a little Polish-born aerialist—and a star—who played the Baltimore date. She went to bed in the circus train on closing night, woke up in Washington and went to the show grounds to find the tents in the air and everything ready for the matinee performance. For the first several stands, nobody could convince

198

her that we had done it all in one morning and that the show did not carry two complete units, "leap-frogging" each other. We took for granted this miraculous "building a new canvas city in a new town every day," but people from other lands who never had seen it happen simply couldn't believe that the "crazy Americans" could do any such thing.

It is a matter of good system. Before the night performance is over, the wild-animal menagerie is loaded onto the first train, along with the cook and dining equipment, and is leaving for the next town while the customers are still on the grounds. Side-show and big-top physical equipment follow on a second train and the last unit to leave town is the performer section which can get to the next stand as late as noon and still be in time to make the matinee.

Everybody was glad to be under canvas. The New York City indoor engagement is profitable and it is the publicity springboard for the show's tour out over the country, but the performers don't like the building in the early springtime where there is difference of temperature in the dressing rooms, the drafty corridors and the arena, the streets and hotels. We don't live in the circus trains for those two early stands. We stay in hotels and rooming houses. The "Garden" variety of head and chest colds is famous, and Polyclinic Hospital across from Madison Square Garden on the 50th Street side has many a circus person as guest during our Manhattan engagement.

With the "Big One" we had beautiful girls from all over the world, but it always struck me that nobody could touch our home-grown variety. The girls from the farms and the small towns were especially good looking and talented. A farm background is a valuable asset to a girl who wants to be a circus performer. She has grown up with animals and she knows about working in all kinds of weather and she doesn't expect the tour to be a plush picnic.

Now although I had been warned to lay off clowning when acts like the Cristianis and Truzzi and Elly Ardelty, an aerial single, were performing, each of them sought me out to put some comedy into their numbers.

Ardelty had quite an entrance. She had a fanfare and a special announcement and she did a beautiful act that finished when she stood on her head in her swinging trapeze. This tiny blonde had class and was unusually graceful, having studied ballet in Europe as have so many other of the best performers.

I worked out a gag with Elly wherein the hobo carefully removes her expensive evening wrap as she prepares to ascend the rigging, stands worried and hopelessly in love as she does the dangerous tricks and is her worshipful slave as she comes down to thunderous applause. Then she passes him by with the merest suggestion of a polite smile as she leaves the arena, and he is heartbroken.

Lucio Cristiani, the riding comedian in that great family act of Italian-born equestrians, came to me early in my first Ringling season and asked me to work my clowning into their routine. One of the things I did was to get a short ladder and when Lucio purposely missed a somersault from one galloping horse to another, running tandem, I would prop the ladder against the horse, climb up and sweep his broad back with a broom so that Lucio would not slip the next time he tried the trick. The rider liked this gag because it gave him time to catch his breath.

Then Massimiliano Truzzi, a great juggler with a rare streak of comedy in his work, approached me. He came waving his arms and talking in some foreign tongue. I thought he was complaining, but I finally tumbled to the fact that he wanted me to do something funny while he worked the act.

I thought up some romantic by-play with his pretty wife, who assisted him. She would give me the eye while Truzzi was doing his best to hold the attention of the crowd, and I would wave at her timidly with my old red bandanna. Then, after Truzzi had dropped a lot of plates he was trying to keep in the air, I would carry an old burlap sack to him and offer to catch the plates he kept dropping. Insulted, he would point an indignant finger as if to say *"Go!,"* and I would leave the ring —looking sad because I had been rebuffed for simply trying to help him.

Valdo suggested that I build up this by-play, so the show made me a little fence—four feet square and sixteen inches high. It had a tiny swinging gate. When Truzzi ordered me out of the ring, I would go to my "castle," carefully reach down and open the gate, step inside and close it. My attitude now changed to one of mild defiance and the whole routine was so ridiculous it amused people.

I used the little portable fence for a victory garden gag, too. In this presentation, I would set up the fence, carefully rake the ground and prepare to plant. I had a couple of paper packages of seeds with me and I was so hungry that I'd keep nibbling away at them. The wallop of the gag was that when the ground finally was ready for planting, the famished planter had eaten all the seeds.

Both Truzzi and Cristiani told me that they had tried on several occasions to thread a little comedy into their acts by using a clown and that even though some of the comics who tried it were imitating my tramp-clown appearance, the laughs never came. This encouraged me to try for more participation routines. One that seemed to go over well I hitched to Roland Tiebor's sea-lion acts. They worked in the rings, but I sat outside where I had built a tiny fire and was warming my hands when I would notice that Tiebor was feeding fish to his clever animals. At that point I produced a little skillet and stood hopefully just outside the circle of sea lions. When the trainer would toss each of them a hunk of fish as a reward for doing a trick, the hungry hobo's confidence would rise and

201

he would appear certain of being included in the feast. Of course it never happened and "Willie" wandered away dejected.

I also worked some comedy into a tightwire act recently by coming out just ahead of the performers and using the wire for a clothesline. On it I hung a ragged bandanna and two or three other equally shabby items. My attitude was one of surprised and offended innocence when the acrobat and his wife showed up and chased me.

In Washington, D.C., my first year with the Ringling show, one of our guests in the back yard was Lord Halifax, the British ambassador. He had watched the afternoon performance and had been brought into the private areas of the circus to see the mechanics of our operation and to meet some of the people. When we shook hands, he said he had seen me when I was in London with the Bertram Mills Circus. The size of our American circus surprised him and he was mighty impressed by George Blood's cook and dining department.

This part of the show is even more efficient today because the old coal-and-wood burners have been replaced by oil-burning stoves mounted permanently on wagons—something we learned from the Army in World War II. This was turn-about and fair play because up to World War II, the military studied the circus and copied its methods of feeding and of transportation. They say that the German army in World War I increased its efficiency by copying circus methods which Kaiser Wilhelm's engineers had seen on the Barnum & Bailey Circus during its five years in Europe, 1897-1902.

We felt the labor shortage as soon as we began the one-day stands. We all felt it because we all had to "double in brass and overalls," so to speak. Candy butchers, ushers, ticket sellers and performers pitched in with the regular workingmen and moved the show. We carried poles, we carried seats, we carried planks; we put up and took down our own dressing tent and we loaded our own trunks.

For this rough work we would change to overalls and we would select a midget to watch our street clothes—left in neat little piles on a spread of canvas carpet in the back yard. Usually the midget was Paul Horompo, and we figured we could trust him with our personal wardrobe because nothing would fit him. Sometimes we put on boots and raincoats and labored in driving rain. It was rough going, but we always managed to move the show and make our towns.

The circus name for this extra work is "cherry pie." When somebody tells you that such-and-such a circus has plenty of "cherry pie" every day, he is not talking about the cookhouse; he is telling you that the show is shorthanded and that everybody does double duty. There is a division of opinion about the origin of this expression. Some say that the way to spell it is "chairy pie" because it refers to the carrying of thousands of folding grandstand chairs. I don't know where the name came from, but I sure do know how it feels in the legs and arms and back, when the manager says, "Boys, we got a lot of cherry pie for you tonight!"

Some of our matinees started late, but we made every town, and there was one I wish we hadn't made. As if the ordinary day-by-day difficulties dished up by trouping in wartime weren't enough, there was a black date on our calendar and it caught us in Cleveland, Ohio.

I was sleeping late in the morning at the Auditorium Hotel a couple of blocks from the circus grounds along the lake-front. This was a three-day stand and I had decided to break the monotony of the circus train by checking into a hotel. The breeze from Lake Erie kept the window shades flapping and this sound woke me. I tried to go back to sleep, but was brought out of bed by the sound of fire sirens and

203

trumpeting elephants. I pulled up the shade and looked down toward the City Hall and there was an elephant running in the street. She had her ears out and her tail up and I knew she was scared. I figured that our elephants had stampeded, but there was something wrong in that reasoning because our elephant boss, Walter McClain, was one of the greatest animal men in the world and never had had a stampede. The animals had the utmost confidence in him and he could teach them to do just about anything except sell tickets.

I pulled on my pants and ran down the hotel corridor to the northwest corner where I could look out the window and see the circus grounds. Somebody's door was open and a maid was in there making up the room. I ran in and looked toward our grounds. Smoke was rolling up and I knew it had to be from the circus. It looked to me as if the side-show tent was on fire.

Anyhow, we were in trouble and I didn't waste time. I ran back to the room, put on my shirt and shoes and raced out. Taking a short cut through an alley, I got to the grounds in record time and saw fire equipment all over the place. I looked toward the front of the show, the flags were flying on the side-show top; then I looked for the menagerie tent, but it was gone. It had burned to the ground.

Moving through a dense crowd, I talked a policeman into letting me through the barrier, but I almost wish I hadn't. There was nothing I could do. The canvas was gone, although the tent's center poles were still standing. Hose was pouring water on piles of smoldering hay, and the circus veterinarian was going around with armed cops, instructing them which caged animals should be put out of their misery.

The elephants were all out of the menagerie. A giraffe had broken loose and had come galloping through the circus main entrance, charging through the ticket gates and into the midway where it was captured. This was the only one we

204

saved; two other giraffes, including a young one, died in the fire.

The stench of burned flesh and the sound of cracking rifles, plus the fact that there was nothing to be done, drove me away, feeling heartbroken. Half our menagerie was gone and this was wartime when no wild animals were being imported. Our elephant herd, usually at the figure of forty-plus, had been reduced in 1941 when ten died of arsenic poisoning in Atlanta. Now I had no idea how many more we had lost.

I went back to the hotel and ordered breakfast, but I couldn't eat anything. Into the public auditorium building, where I had appeared with many a winter circus under Grotto auspices, but now empty, they were leading some of our elephants. One had its skin hanging in strips. I went out into the street. Some of these elephants had inhaled flame and their lungs were seared, and there was a kind of breathless rumbling as they stood there suffering. Circus people love all the animals, but there is something very special about the "bulls," as elephants—regardless of sex—are called. And, of course, the horses.

In this fire, the origin of which never was determined, we lost five elephants, all our camels and most of the llamas, two giraffes and a lot of cage exhibits. Mayor Frank Lausche, now Ohio governor, came down to the show grounds with tears in his eyes and offered us the sympathy of his city and the use of the auditorium to hospitalize our injured elephants.

There had been no elephant stampede. Those wonderful bulls had either pulled their chains and walked away from the fire or had waited patiently for their keepers to come and get them out of the flaming straw and the burning canvas overhead. The menagerie boys didn't fail them although some of the elephants were burned beyond recovery by the time they got out.

Our animal men were burned from going into that blazing tent to save their animals. We cancelled the matinee, but did a quick clean-up job and corralled what was left of the menagerie and opened the gates on time for an evening show. Our disaster had one redeeming aspect—it made front-page news, and business was good there as people flocked to see what had happened and to admire the "show must go on" spirit of the troupe. As they sauntered through the wild-animal menagerie that night, they saw McClain and his men putting salve on the burned places of the elephants who had been saved—a new kind of medicine which had been sent by plane to the show that afternoon. Because the gates were not open to the public at noontime, nobody had been caught in this fire except our own, and there was no panic such as in the Hartford fire when the circus people outside couldn't get inside to help evacuate the tent because the crowd stampeded in all directions.

Our next stand was Akron, where we erected the previous year's menagerie tent, shipped to us from winter quarters. We had lost a good many animals, but still carried far more than any other circus on the road. It was an interesting coincidence that after the Hartford fire, the first stand we made was Akron again.

At the end of the 1942 tour, the circus changed management. John Ringling North took a leave-of-absence; his younger brother, Henry, went into the Navy; and Robert Ringling, son of one of the founders, became president. George Smith returned as the show's general manager, and Ed Kelly became his assistant. Pat Valdo remained as personnel director. Johnny North had preferred the more intimate presentation afforded by holding the big top to a three-ring size, but Bob Ringling returned it to the traditional three-rings-and-two stages and decided to hold full-scale rehearsals at winter quarters. I never had been to Sarasota, but one day while I was visiting my family in Lafayette, Indiana, the New

York Central agent notified me that he was holding a ticket for me from Lafayette to Sarasota, and I went.

Sarasota is a pretty place on the west coast of Florida, and in spite of the fact that it has been growing steadily and is filled with tourist trade in the winter months, it manages to retain a good deal of small-town flavor. Circus winter quarters is three miles east of the city and is an impressive layout. There are buildings for the animals, and connecting with them are outdoor cages and pens where they can take advantage of good weather and be on exhibition zoo-fashion. The circus has general offices, a publicity building, a big dining hall, a hospital; shops for painting wagons and railroad cars, for woodworking, canvas-making, wardrobe, machinery; a dormitory for workingmen; circular "ring barns" where riding acts can practice, portable steel arenas for rehearsing the wild-animal acts and just about everything you could think of that is needed to get the big show ready for the next tour. Thousands of people visit the winter quarters to see the people and the animals in rehearsal and to get a good look at the circus with its glamour down, dressed in practice clothes and hard at work.

In a large open space near the stables is an oval-shaped, open arena the dimensions of the Madison Square Garden arena. This is where the program is put together and where the whole show shapes up to the way it will be by the time we start rolling north at the end of March for the opening date in New York. A good many circus performers own their own homes in and around Sarasota, and those who are aerialists usually have their rigging set up in their yards. Circus atmosphere is all over town and the natives don't think anything of it if they walk out of a corner drugstore and see somebody walking on his hands.

I checked into a hotel and took a cab to winter quarters, wondering why they would want me for rehearsals—especially since I worked my clowning into the program piecemeal and did not appear in clown "production" numbers. John Murray Anderson was busy planning the "spec," which turned out to be a nostalgic replica of the old-time parade. No circus had marched in the streets for many years and even though this one would be under the tent, it was a nice novelty and contained the beautiful old carved bandwagon that had toured Europe with the Barnum & Bailey Circus at the turn of the century, an old steam calliope and several ancient tableau wagons as well. Anderson saw me and signaled. "Now, Mr. Kelly," he began, "I want you to go into 'spec' this year."

My face must have fallen a foot because he hastened to add, "Now, don't worry. You won't have to change your costume."

What I finally wound up doing in the parade number, called "Hold Your Horses," was ride on a little fire cart with Prince Paul, a midget driver.

Another of our handsome production numbers was a procession called "Let Freedom Ring," heavy on patriotism and red, white and blue. For finale numbers during the war years we'd have giant-size cloth pictures of the President and enormous American flags that unfolded in sections from the thirty-foot-long trains of circus girls who climbed lofty rigging at the ends and center of the huge tent. Another finale, the year after the war, was called "Drums of Victory" and featured a giant-size model of the Statue of Liberty for a finishing thrill.

1943 was one of those rare seasons when the circus met no disasters, did good business—especially in the industrial areas where payrolls were heavy and people were anxious to forget the war news by spending a few hours in a land of make-believe. Of course, the labor shortage was worse than ever, but we were accustomed to a steady diet of "cherry pie" now and took it in our stride.

We did have a couple of minor difficulties, both in the Washington stand. A sudden windstorm made the quarter poles dance, and for a minute Leonard Aylesworth, the boss canvasman, thought the big top was going to go. A hole or two ripped in the canvas where quarter poles slipped their moorings and punched through was the total damage.

But one night just after the performance was under way, our people started being sick and dropping like flies all over the back yard. Nobody collapsed in the big top; all who weren't stricken before they went in managed to get through their acts and conceal their condition until they were out of the tent. Some kind of food poisoning was responsible, but it never was tracked down because the whole troupe had all eaten the same dinner in the dining tent and only about a third of the troupe was affected. That was the night Merle Evans had to break his twenty-three-year record of never leaving the bandstand during a performance. He knew he was going to be sick, but he waited until the last minute before he staggered off the stand. Actually he was gone for only a couple of minutes when he heard something in the music that didn't suit him, and he climbed back up to finish the program.

So many performers were sick that there were some holes in the show, but they were covered up cleverly and the public knew nothing of our epidemic until the morning-paper headlines told the story. About one hundred of our company wound up in a hospital about a mile from the circus grounds, taxing it over its capacity. Nearly everybody was able to leave next day, however, and the show went on as usual.

We were getting no acts now from Europe or Asia and relied on Mexico, Central and South America for importations. I remember that when the war was new and we were in our Boston stand, a couple of men came quietly to the dressing room and asked for Fritz Schultz. He was asleep in his chair at the time. They woke him up and talked with him in low voices and shortly thereafter Fritz was packing his trunk. These were federal agents and they interned Schultz for the duration of the war because he was a German national and had five brothers in the Nazi army. Fritz was a wild-animal trainer and had come to this country about four years earlier with three wonderful wild-animal acts trained and owned by a Frenchman named Alfred Court. I never saw Schultz again.

We had a couple of Japanese with the show at the start of the war—a man and his son, and even though they were English-born and strangers to Japan, they were taken away too. I heard, however, that they weren't interned for long, but were permitted to go to work for the express company in Sarasota after a short period.

Except for whatever pull they get from blood-ties, a lot of foreign-born troupers in our business really haven't any country except the circus itself. Born in one country, moved the next week to another, half around the world and back by the time they are grown up, these folks don't belong much anywhere but in a community made up of tents and wagons and animals and bands and railroad trains that keep them on the move all the time.

Press agent Bill Fields told us one night not long ago, in New York City, that a lot of the United Nations people were in the house. They came from countries that of course have circuses, but I'm sure they never before saw anything like the "Big One."

We have all races, religions, sizes and shapes with the circus. We have arguments and bad feeling from time to time, but when just "keeping the show on the road" is as tough a job as it is in the outdoor branch of show business, there is mighty little time for beefing and for worrying about the people you work beside.

I have watched the kids grow up around the show. Their parents came from Italy, Germany, Sweden, Russia, Mexico,

France, England, Ireland, Scotland and Wales; from the South American countries, India, Africa, China, Japan. The kids play together and when they start to become circus performers, they work together and they don't have any prejudice unless they learn it from the old folks. The big percentage of these "imports," as the acts from foreign countries are called, take out their citizenship papers; their children all learn English and before long most of their ties with whatever their folks brought from other places have disappeared.

We had one flying act called the Otaris. These people came from Russia in the early nineteen thirties. They had a freak rigging shaped like a maltese cross and they flew in two separate directions for a startling effect. By the time World War II came along, they were American citizens and had four boys enlisted for Uncle Sam. They didn't have to be called; they volunteered, and one of the boys was killed on the Normandy beachhead on D-Day. This left a hole in the company when the war was over and the family had put the flying-return act into the air again. So Pop Otari, almost seventy, but slim as a boy and looking like a young man when he was in the air, went back into the routine to fill the gap left by the lost boy. A magazine writer did a story about him and called it "The Daring Old Man on the Flying Trapeze."

The circus management now frowned upon featured acts and clowns working for the winter circuses in cities where we would be bringing the same people back with the "Big One" a few months later. But there was plenty of night-club work as well as dates in war-production centers.

I did my cartoon act in the plants all around Cleveland —such places as the Thompson Products Company and the Cleveland Bronze Company—and I loved to keep these dates. Sometimes they were after midnight when shifts changed. One was at three in the morning. We'd have a little platform or small stage where there would be a piano and a master of ceremonies. Most of the audiences were girls and I would wait until they were all seated before bursting into the room and starting to sweep the aisles. Then I would stop suddenly and lean on the broom lost in love with some pretty female. This always seemed to go across well and get the act off to a good start.

The next edition of the circus had "Panto's Paradise" for a feature. I had instructions to stop in New York City en route to Sarasota and get a mate to my costume for whoever would be my double for the hobo's dream. I went to Brooks Costume Company and hung up my coat and pants. They had a tough time duplicating this outfit. Finally, with ripping, tearing, trampling, blow-torching and painting they came up with something that resembled my disreputable wardrobe. I tried it on, but it didn't feel like my own suit, by now almost a part of my skin, and I decided to let my double have the new outfit. I picked out two green shirts, the first major change I had made in my costume in some years.

When Bob Ringling saw them, he was delighted. "Emmett," he said, "whatever you do you must never get away from that green shirt. It goes with your name and is a nice touch of color to relieve the drabness—just enough."

I decided then to use a clothespin for a tie clasp and I still use it.

My shoes had been bought in London and I went to Leroy's to have them copied. This duplicate pair cost the show sixty-five dollars. Now came the hard part—trying to find someone my size and who could double for me in that one-dream scene. I finally picked Joe Siegrist, an aerialist who was my size. Even the shoes fitted him perfectly and I asked him to take good care of them. I figured I could use them for a spare set after this tour and that is the way it worked out. Bob Ringling gave them to me and I sent my old pair back to Indiana where my sister retired them for me in a trunk along with my first hobo coat and pants. The only thing I still wear from the early outfit is the dollar derby I have had for twenty-one years.

Earl "Skater" Reynolds, who was responsible for most of the roller-skating thrill acts and who had taught what must have been half the kids in northern Indiana to perform on wheels, brought to the 1945 circus two girl acts. The fill-in or understudy girl was named Mildred Richey and she caught my eye from the start. She had brown hair, blue eyes and an appealingly cute way about her.

By the time we opened in the Garden, I was sharing a dressing room with the bandmaster on arena level where the acts lined up to go in and I found myself waiting to get a glimpse of Mildred when I knew it was time for her to go on. Gradually, from an exchange of smiles and bits of conversation, we started seeing each other frequently. I'd take her out to dinner after the night show and then back to her apartment where she roomed with her sister and another girl. There, if I was lucky, I'd kiss her good night and then walk slowly back to my hotel, really in love for the second time in my life.

I worried for fear that maybe this girl just had stars in her eyes and liked me because I was featured in the show. I was getting a lot of publicity and the other clowns ribbed me about being a star. It was all good-natured, and Paul Jung said to me: "Emmett, you are helping to elevate clowning and we are all for you."

Most of all, I worried about the difference in Mildred's and my ages. Although she was eighteen, she felt strongly that age made no difference. What encouraged me further was the fact that my father had been married happily with a greater age span between him and my mother than there would be between Mildred and me. Mildred's mother came on to visit her and she seemed to approve of me. She, too, said that the age matter was of no concern if we were really in love, but since Mildred was under age she would have to go with us to buy the license. I proposed and was accepted, and like wildfire the news was all over the show that "our bum" was engaged to be married.

We bought the license and I asked the clerk to keep it out of the papers for the time being. The question now was when we would be married and where. Roland Butler was the head press agent that year and he said to me, "Let's do this right; you should be married in the ring."

Both being troupers, we readily agreed. Butler and a good "stunt" press agent, Hal Olver, started to work up the event. This was not the first time that circus performers had been married in the arena. Years before, in the old Garden downtown, a clown named LaPearl had been married in full costume, with the rest of the performers in their show wardrobe and with an elaborate wedding supper for the New York press and other guests after the ceremony.

Mildred's and my wedding was to be less spectacular. No circus wardrobe and no big party; just the ceremony taking place in the center ring between matinee and evening performance. A prominent friend of Bob Ringling's, Judge Frankenthaler, was to marry us, but he objected to doing it in the circus ring. We were lined up and waiting for him, and the troupe was scattered around the building in the seats for several minutes before we were told that the judge wanted to do the actual marrying in the office instead of in the arena. That is the way it was done. After the ceremony in the office, we went out into the ring and stood as though the wedding were taking place there. This was for the photographers. There was nobody to take the judge's place, however, so Butler asked one of the publicity men, who was dressed in a dark blue suit and who looked serious enough to be a preacher, if he would be the stand-in.

214

One night a few days after the wedding, Mildred's sister came to my dressing room at show time and said my wife was very ill. She had bad cramps and we brought her across the street to Polyclinic Hospital where the doctors said it was acute appendicitis. Mildred was operated on at once, and I spent my time worrying and running back and forth between the Garden and the Hospital until she was safely out of the woods.

After that operation my bride seemed strange and unhappy. The doctor saw her every day at our hotel, and assured me that Mildred was perfectly all right, but she was different to me. I couldn't get her to tell me what could be wrong. Finally she said she wanted to make a trip home to see her mother and to rest for a week or so and I consented. For a while I'd get letters; then for a long stretch there was no letter.

I wrote to her mother, who replied that Mildred had been seeing a boy she had gone with before she had married me. Near the end of the New York circus engagement she returned, and at the station seemed glad to see me. That night Robert Ringling was having a big party for the circus personnel in the ballroom of the Hotel New Yorker, but Mildred said she didn't want to go.

That upset me and I told her, "They are expecting you and it will be awkward for me if I show up without you."

I finally did go without her, but it was painful and embarrassing and I determined to talk things out that evening. The upshot of our discussion was an agreement to be divorced. She maintained that she had made a grave mistake, and believed she was in love with a boy back home. I did not wish to hold her against her will, so regretfully I agreed to a divorce.

Now my circus "family" was reduced again to just "Willie" and me. I was more melancholy than my hobo clown

215

character and began to wonder why I wasn't lucky at cards.

If I was thinking of my own tragedy then, I was shortly to participate in a much greater one. One day, when I sat down on my trunk in the circus dressing tent and pulled off my comic, oversize shoes, the soles were blistered from walking through hot ashes. For this was July 6, 1944, the day the big top burned down.

I felt as though I had lived a lifetime in the seven minutes of that calamity. And my nerves were jumping after having been almost killed by one of the show's giant-size caterpillars which had swung around to pull an electric-light plant away from the crowd to avoid an explosion in the midst of panic-stricken people.

I was bone-weary, but I felt a great relief when another clown, Willie Mosier, came into the tent and said, "Thank God! They say nobody was caught in the big top; I think they all got out safe."

But Willie was mistaken about that. He was wrong by a count of one hundred sixty-eight.

The day had started for me like most other circus days. Hartford, Connecticut, usually is a one-day stand, but it had been booked for two days that year. Because of labor shortage and other difficulties in the war days, we eased the customary schedule and played longer in some of the bigger cities. Money was plentiful and business was good enough to back up this kind of booking.

I left the circus trains late in the morning, did some shopping downtown and then went to the show grounds. I opened my trunk, hung up my costume and arranged my grease paint and other makeup materials. Other performers were drifting in one by one, but the clowns waited until the last minute to make up because the day was hot as blazes.

When one forty-five rolled around the bugler blew first-call on his cornet. I dressed in my ragged, hobo costume and made up my face complete with the putty nose, hoping it wouldn't melt in the blistering heat.

The performance began at two-fifteen and my first appearance came early in the show. Another clown and I were to do a bit where we stood in the center ring directly under the Wallenda troupe's high-wire and held a tiny handkerchief in which to catch them if they fell from a spectacular three-high human pyramid on the wire.

But the performance always began with the wild animal acts. As I put the finishing touches on my face, I could hear the band playing for the finish of the animal display and then going into the Wallenda waltz music. At that instant, somebody ran past the dressing tent, yelling "Fire!"

That word is the all-time nightmare of circus business. I ran outside and saw smoke curling up from the end of the main tent nearest the midway or what we call the "front of the show." At first, I thought it might be the side-show tent. Then I thought of the menagerie, but I remembered that since space was limited on the Hartford layout, we had corralled the cages and elephants and enclosed them with canvas side-wall. We had not put the menagerie tent over them for this date.

I hoped it might be only a straw fire in the menagerie area, but the smoke was too black for a straw fire. It looked more like the burning of the menagerie top in Cleveland two years before this.

Later I realized that I was merely doing some quick wishful thinking when I thought the fire was coming from the side-show or the wild-animal area. Anything but the big top. That is the thing circus people dread above all else, since it involves the public and includes so many children.

But it was the big top.

I was trying to run and I was making poor headway in my big, flapping clown shoes. Suddenly I noticed that I was

217

carrying a water bucket that I had grabbed when I left the dressing tent where every performer has a bucket of wash water beside his trunk.

There was nothing I could do with it because the tent was burning too high from the ground, and the flame was spreading. I could hear the grandstand chairs slamming inside the tent as people stampeded down onto the hippodrome track and made for the exits. Some were jumping off the top rows of the grandstand and bleacher seats, a distance of twelve feet, to the ground outside, and at one place a couple of quick-thinking circus workingmen had pulled the canvas sidewall out tight to make a sort of slanting chute that people could slide down.

But most of the crowd was pouring through the exits and it soon became a panic. I tried to get into the tent, but there was no chance to break through that mass of frightened people. Some of them, as soon as they were outside and in the clear, must have remembered people they had left inside because many were trying to push back into the tent. I fought these bottlenecks as well as I could, yelling at the top of my lungs: "Go on! You can't get back in there! Keep moving, keep moving!"

At every jammed exit, circus people were busy doing the same thing. It was a frantic, milling mob. I remember one little girl who came out crying for her mother. I grabbed her away from the crowd and said: "Listen, honey—listen to the old clown. You go way over there to that victory garden and wait for your mommy. She'll come along soon."

The last I saw of her she was trotting over to the edge of the show grounds where a victory garden plot was. I never learned if she found her mother but it was a long time before I could stop dreaming about her.

Sparks were flying and the heat drove us back. It was hard to push the people away from the tent. The circus fire wagons were throwing water, but it was evident now that no-body could put out that fire. The big top was a goner. The canvas was nearly all burned away now and the center poles were crashing one by one. Merle Evans and his musicians had kept on playing until the tent was afire overhead, and they had jumped off the bandstand just before a quarter-pole fell flaming into the stand.

May Kovar, a British lion tamer, had been in the big cage when the fire started, sending her animals into the de-livery chutes as always at the end of the act. She knew what might happen if one of her cats got away when the steel arena crashed, and she stayed until the last one was out. She stuck there at her own risk like the trouper she was and barely got out with her life.

The circus electric-light plants are in big wagons and flames were licking at one of them which was parked a few feet from the big top. People were all around it and wouldn't move. I grabbed a man with his coat over his arm. "Good God! Come with me! This thing is liable to blow up!" I hol-lered into his ear. We ran to the horse troughs, filled four buckets and threw the water on the fire. At that moment, I nearly got it. One of the caterpillar tractors came rumbling along to get that wagon—to hook on and pull it away from the crowd. It was almost on top of me before I realized what was happening, and as it swung around it didn't miss running over me by more than an inch.

City fire equipment had arrived by now, and water was being poured onto the big-top area so it would cool enough for firemen to go in. There was so much smoke and so much confusion outside it was impossible to tell whether anybody might have been left in there. Firemen and police now were pushing everybody back. All of us circus people were ordered away from the smoking rubble that a few minutes before had been the biggest spread of canvas in the world. I could hardly

219

see, my eyes were smarting so from the smoke. I had a few places on my face and hands burned from sparks, but I didn't feel them then. I stumbled off to the dressing tent where I found some of our men busy putting out small fires that flying sparks had started.

This was when Willie Mosier came in and said he was pretty sure that nobody had been caught under the big top. Some of our people were bruised and burned from the rescue work, but all seemed to be present. Most of them had got out the performers' entrance at the far end of the tent, on either side of the bandstand. Later, it was discovered that very few spectators had used these exits. In a panic, it seems to be the nature of people to try to go out the way they came in. The public had not come into the tent through the performers' entrance and they paid no attention to it as a means of getting out. Those who escaped by that route had followed the directions of the circus people.

The big top had caught fire at a time when few performers were working, since the Wallendas performed alone. Nothing took place anywhere else in the tent to distract the attention of the audience from this thriller. If the fire had occurred a few minutes later, the three rings, two stages and the entire hippodrome oval would have been crowded with elephants and horses and hundreds of performers and the tragedy would have been far worse.

So I sat down now and removed my shoes and put my feet into a bucket of water while bathing my eyes and trying to clean my face. I felt a great relief at what Willie had said, but I knew we had lost the big top and all the aerial rigging and the seats, and that this was wartime when it would be mighty hard to get any replacement materials.

We sat around without saying much. Most of us were thinking about how we'd be out of work if the show went off the road. Finally, some of the boys began to be nervous. "Why won't the police and firemen allow us near the fire area?" somebody asked. This was only a few minutes after the start of the fire but it seemed much longer to everybody in that dressing tent.

Then we heard a sound that froze us all. The long, thin wail of an ambulance siren. Another and another and another until the air was filled with the sound. We knew then. We knew that something a lot more precious than canvas and rope and hardware and the 1944 tour had been lost.

I went outside the tent and the smell of burned flesh was in the air. They were carrying bodies from where the grand-stands and bleacher seats had been. Doctors and nurses and first-aid people in white jackets were everywhere. The Hart-ford Red Cross disaster group, police and firemen did a big job well, but the toll of dead and dying mounted so fast that emergency crews were called in from surrounding cities. It was plainly a major disaster, and some returned soldiers there that afternoon said later that they had not seen anything worse in towns where they had been under bombs.

The police and firemen and ambulance and Red Cross units had a system working and they still kept everybody else back. I went to the dressing tent again and told the guys the bad news. Most of them had sensed it when they'd heard the ambulances. I don't recall that anybody said a word; they just sat there. Before long, Pat Valdo, head of all our performing personnel and a clown once himself, came in to tell us that we were not to leave the premises. We sat and waited while the news got worse and worse.

We heard now that five of our main men had been ar-rested on technical charges—the chief electrician, the super-intendent of seats, the boss canvasman, the general manager and the vice-president. Robert Ringling was president that year, but he was not in Hartford. He had left the show for a few days and was in Chicago on business, so they arrested the next highest in command, James Haley.

We were puzzled when we heard this. Did they think one of our own men was responsible for setting the fire? Why arrest five—could they think that *five* men had done it? Someone recalled then that after the Coconut Grove night-club fire in Boston, a year or so before this, the owners had served prison sentences after conviction on charges of criminal negligence. But at least one of those men had a police record and they were not the kind of people that our men were. We knew our top officials and department heads were all reliable men of good reputation. We were completely baffled.

Nobody, however, ever found out for certain how the fire started. It didn't start at ground level or it could have been extinguished quickly as it crept up the canvas sidewall. We always had men stationed at intervals around the main tent, and under the seats and we had water wagons and fire extinguishers on the grounds. That fire somehow began up in the main spread of the canvas. Years later, a mental patient in Ohio claimed he had been employed by the circus for a few days in 1944 and that he had set the tent on fire for a thrill. His story sounded possible, but he was unreliable on other subjects and nobody ever could be sure.

Toward the end of the longest afternoon of my life, we were told that we were free to go to the trains or to hotels where some of the troupe had checked in the night before to get away from the mosquitoes and heat of the sleeping cars. We were ordered to leave our trunks, costumes and everything else right there in the tent. It looked as though we might be stranded here indefinitely. The next day's town was to be Springfield, Massachusetts. We knew we'd never make that date or any other on the immediate itinerary, and we began to wonder if we'd ever play another town anywhere.

222

Leaving the show grounds, I walked past the ruins of the big top and saw some charred shoes and part of a clown doll lying on what had been the hippodrome track. That moment was when the tension of the past hours broke over me in a wave and I couldn't keep from crying any longer.

I didn't want to spend another hot night on the train, so I tried to get a room in a hotel. The town now was jammed with newspaper and radio and picture magazine people from New York City and from some of the large New England towns. There were no rooms available, but Harold Nicholson and another man had a twin-bed room in a good hotel and they offered to put the beds together so I could bunk in with them.

In the lobby of the Bond Hotel sat quite a few of our people. They weren't talking or reading papers; they were just sitting still and looking into space—remembering the most awful seven or eight minutes in the whole history of circus business.

We had been through wind and rain and mud, and we had seen wild animals on the loose and railroad wrecks and fires and all the other misfortunes that are part of outdoor trouping. All these things we were familiar with. But always before, in circus catastrophes, the people who died or got hurt had been mostly our own. The terrible thing about the Hartford fire was that the victims had been our customers, and that so many of them were kids.

It was evening now and word came that the armory was filled with bodies and long lines of sorrowing friends and relatives trying to make identifications. One pretty little girl never was identified. When all had been accounted for, this child, dead from burns, but her face without any disfigurement, remained. Nobody ever claimed her to this day although her picture ran in every newspaper in the United States and Canada. The Hartford Fire Department buried the little body, and on each anniversary of the disaster it places flowers on her grave.

The city that night was in a state of shock. It seemed that almost every family in town knew somebody who had lost a friend or a relative or had suffered themselves. The people did not think we had burned down on purpose, but there was an undercurrent of feeling about it nevertheless. We were outsiders who had come to town and advertised that we were in the business of making people happy. And we were Ringling Brothers and Barnum & Bailey—the biggest thing of its kind in the world. It was something that just couldn't happen. But it did.

I went into the bar and ordered a beer. A few of our people were there, but nobody was doing any talking—only the bartender who felt sorry for us and tried to cheer us up by saying that everybody knew the circus wasn't to blame.

I went out and walked alone in the sticky-hot night. Newsboys were yelling "Extra!," but I didn't want to read a paper; I had seen enough. Most of the papers and the radio people, especially in Hartford, treated us fairly, but there was a paper in another Connecticut town that shot a picture of our officials right after they were released on bail the morning after the fire. Sleepless and mussed and unshaven they were, as anybody would be under the circumstances. The caption that paper had over the picture was: THEY SAVED THEIR ANIMALS.

It was an unfair thing to do and it hurt. Our people had not done anything to save the animals from the fire. The main tent had caught fire not far from the animal menagerie, but whatever breeze there was had spread the flame in the other direction. The circus people had worked to get the customers out of the big top, not their animals out of the menagerie corral—which wasn't on fire at any time.

One of the charges against our officials was that they had been careless in regard to sufficient exits and particularly in allowing the portable wild-animal delivery tunnel, about waist-high but with steps and a bridge running over it, to block the hippodrome track even for the limited time needed to get the animals in and out of the steel performing arena from their cages outside the tent.

There are fire hazards in theatres, hotels, stores, factories and even in private homes and nobody puts them there on purpose. They aren't recognized as dangerous until a fire starts and panic sets in and these obstacles become death traps. It was that way in the circus fire. We had the identical setup in Hartford that we had in all the other cities on the route. And the circus had been inspected by the fire department, as usual, before our first performance. On the day before we came to town, our "twenty-four-hour man" had taken the extra precaution of cutting a field of high grass next to the grounds because he noticed that it was dry and might make trouble if it caught fire.

I walked along in the night and started to worry about myself now. This year had given me my first big break since coming to the "Big One." The principal production number or spectacle in 1944 was called "Panto's Paradise" and it was presented as the dream of a hobo who fell asleep and dreamed of a vast procession of people and animals, all dressed in glittering gems and costumes, that filled the rings, stages and the track. I used a double for this because I was supposed to be dreaming about myself surrounded with beautiful girls atop a gorgeous float pulled by elephants at the very end of the parade. The "hobo" who fell asleep at the start of it all was my size and had costume and makeup as nearly like mine as possible.

This was the first time in half a century or so that a circus had singled out one clown for feature attention in general publicity. Naturally I was very proud of "Panto's Paradise," but now I decided it really had been a dream as far as I was

225

concerned—a dream I had waked from when somebody yelled "Fire!" The tramp clown was out of work and here it was only July, the middle part of the tour. I decided that next day I would telephone an agent named Charlie Allen in New York to ask his advice.

Next morning I ran into Allen Lester, one of our publicity men, in the hotel lobby who said, "Emmett, that's quite a picture of you on page one of the *Boston Globe*."

I hadn't seen it because I hadn't wanted to read any papers at all. An amateur photographer had taken his camera with him to the circus and had snapped me as I was hurrying along in my tramp outfit and sad expression and with a water bucket in my hand. The picture was syndicated widely and was used by *Life* as its "picture of the week."

That morning after the fire I telephoned the agent in New York. He said he could book me right away with a USO troupe leaving for Panama, and I said I'd let him know. The death toll kept rising with every newspaper edition that hit the street. Hundreds who had lived through the fire were badly burned, and in some cases maimed for life. I began to feel that it was really "curtains" for the circus, but suddenly word came that the whole troupe was to stay intact and await developments. This meant a company of over one thousand and we were on full pay. This was encouraging and I turned down the Panama booking.

Just about the only cheerful thought I had all week was that we had not burned down in Providence, Rhode Island, two days earlier. On the Fourth of July there, we had played to a packed matinee with half again as many people attending as had been under the tent at Hartford. There have been many tragedies in theatres and other public places where loss of life exceeded the Hartford total, but so many in our big top were children. That made it heartbreaking, and unfortunately for the circus it increased the news value of a story that wound

226

up among the ten biggest of the year—despite the fact that it had to compete with a war. A newspaper photographer who got a picture of the charred oval of the big-top area from an airplane won a national prize with it under the title: NO CIRCUS TODAY.

The circus fire received so much publicity that most folks took it for granted that this was the first time a circus main tent ever had been destroyed by fire. But it had happened before—once in Schenectady, New York, in 1912; once in Sterling, Illinois; and one time in Columbus, Georgia. In none of these previous fires, however, had any people been hurt; they had happened when the performance was not going on. Walking the streets alone that night in Hartford, I held out little hope that we could come back from this one.

Time passed slowly while we sat around and waited. The circus sat like a stricken, silent giant on the Hartford lot. The burned area was roped off and under guard. Our management and its attorneys were meeting with state and city officials to decide the immediate future of the show. So now, instead of taking bankruptcy and running out, the circus agreed to shoulder a huge burden, no matter who was to blame for the fire, and to abide by the decisions of a committee that would be set up to settle all fire claims.

This eventually exceeded four million dollars and took nearly eight years to pay off. And the only way this money could be raised was from circus operating profits in the future.

We had last year's main tent, always carried for emergencies like fires and blow-downs, but we all knew that never again would the "Big One" put another piece of canvas in the air unless it was flameproof. No show had flameproof canvas in those days. It was only waterproofed, and quite a fuss was made of the fact that in weatherproofing circus canvas a combination of paraffin and gasoline was used. All outdoor shows used this method and did it at winter quarters in ad-

227

vance of the road tours. The canvas was spread out on the ground and men with long-handled brushes spread the mixture over the cloth. When it dried, of course the gasoline evaporated, but "gasoline" is a word with fire in it and a lot of readers thought we had been careless and carried highly inflammable canvas.

For many years, theatrical companies had been using a flameproofing solution that was put on scenery. It was pretty good for that, but useless on cloth that was folded and unfolded and handled in all kinds of weather every day of the tour. In 1944, there was a new flameproofing process which we could not get because it was restricted to use by military authorities. Cloth treated with this method will burn, but not burst into flame and the fire will not spread. When it is old and tattered, it is as flame-resistant as ever. When we went out under canvas again in 1945, we had managed to get enough of it for our tents, and we still use it today.

None of the show's quarter-million-dollar wardrobe had been hurt in the Hartford fire. The props and rigging and other equipment we had lost could be rebuilt quickly. But we had no tent and no seats. Of course we could go to winter quarters and take our time about getting ready for the next spring, but we all knew that was no good. What we had to do somehow was get up off our knees out of the ashes of the worst circus disaster of all time, put the show on the road again in a hurry and shoulder the overwhelming burden that was sure to come from the hundreds of fire claims. If we could do all this, we might go a long way toward restoring public confidence in the old slogan that "the show must go on." We weren't sure we could do it, but we wanted to try.

When we got orders to move, everybody pitched in. We went through the ruins of the big top and salvaged some valuable metal. Even so, the aerial acts had to build new rigging and they built it themselves in the shops at winter quarters in

Sarasota, where our trains streaked in record time after we pulled out of Hartford.

I could not see into the future where brighter days for the circus and personal triumphs for me lay ahead along the winding trail of the red wagons. I can't say I was too optimistic right then, but we were getting up off the floor and coming back fighting. Newspapers in Tampa and Miami and other cities sent reporters and photographers to winter quarters where a great job of teamwork was under way.

Our traffic manager went to work to set up a route for us to play for the rest of the season under the open sky—in ball parks, stadiums and fair grounds. In such places, we needed no tent and of course the seats were there already. It was a makeshift way of doing things for a show of our size and it had plenty of disadvantages, but it showed the public that we weren't whipped.

One month from the date of the fire, we opened again in the Rubber Bowl at Akron, Ohio. Nobody had lost a day's pay. Keeping more than a thousand people on full pay during time lost through an accident was something new in show business. And the arbitration board that was set up in Hartford to handle the claims of injured people became a model of its kind. Whether or not anybody had any right to blame the circus for the fire, the fact remained that the victims had been our customers on our property, and we faced up to it.

All these things made me proud of the "Big One." If I never knew it before, I knew now that we had every reason to call ourselves "The Greatest Show on Earth."

Of all the dates we played under the open sky following the Hartford fire, the toughest to work was Chicago. There, we set up in Soldier Field and it was the first time the circus ever looked small. That place is so huge that we used only a piece of it and the seats went so high that people in the upper areas sat higher than our aerial acts and actually could look

229

down on them. In the bright sun, I had trouble working in the seats because the sun reflected in my eyes from the white shirts and dresses and from the light-colored cement. We had a sad loss to the "alley" during that engagement. Old Danny McPride, a fine man and one of our best clowns, fell dead as he left the arena and started for the dressing tent. I still can see Danny in his clown suit and makeup, lying on the ground with his little pet dog whimpering and licking his face.

The "Big One" came back strong from the fire and one of the highlights of the next season was our parade on the streets of New York for the Seventh War Loan. To make a parade, circuses need a great many heavy or "work" horses—the Belgians and Percherons and Clydes. After street parades were discontinued, the shows sold their work horses and substituted trucks for the hauling of the wagons from the railroad yards to the exhibition grounds and back again. But that year, 1945, we were carrying a good many heavy horses purely for purposes of exhibition and so we were able to put out an impressive march. New York hadn't seen anything like it for twenty-five years and it was all a big success. Douglas Leigh, foremost of the New York outdoor advertising men, contributed all the signs relating to the purpose of the parade and our units all carried them in the parade which lined up on 49th Street, went down 8th Avenue to 34th Street, crossed over and came back up Broadway. When the first of our three bandwagons wheeled into Times Square with the brass pouring out that exciting circus music which sounds like nothing else in this world, it was something to remember.

That was the day a photographer put a child in my arms for a picture and the kid took one look at me and bellowed. That mournful shot of the two of us made all the papers coast to coast.

I woke up one late morning during our Garden engagement and heard the sirens all blowing. It was V-E Day. I dressed and went to Times Square, but the crowd was so thick I had to give it up. I felt mighty good about it, but my boy was in the South Pacific and there was still plenty of trouble out there.

My folks were visiting me at the circus in Indianapolis when V-J Day arrived. We were expecting the news and the circus was wondering if it should cancel the date and pack up for fear that when the great news was flashed the crowd might get out of hand and run wild. But we had a hard rainstorm and the crowd was small and everything was orderly. I felt wonderful because I knew now that my sailor son was going to get back alive.

Later during that tour a young man came to see me and reminded me that at some night club I had drawn a picture of myself, autographed it and given it to him. "I was on a carrier that was sunk and that picture was tacked on the wall of my bunk," he explained. "I was very proud of it and would like another because now it is at the bottom of the sea."

I was happy to sit right down and draw him a fresh one —happy that he wasn't where the other picture had gone.

Now even though the war was over, circus trouping was tough as ever. Some of our top officials including Manager George Smith were in prison for eight months and twenty days, convicted on technical manslaughter charges at Hartford. We felt extremely bitter about this. It made about as much sense to us as if the president of a university and his trustees had been sent to jail because people were killed when the seats collapsed during a basketball game, an accident that actually happened.

We missed these men, but Ed Kelly did a great job of keeping the "old rag" in the air, as the big top is called— even when it is brand new. I still have a picture of him in my mind—working from early morning until late at night in all kinds of weather with his first assistant, Lloyd Morgan, his jaw set against every obstacle and his pocket full of dollar bills to peel off on the spot for extra work done daily by the "cherry pie" crowd. For a while, we even had some of the circus girls helping with the grandstand chairs and some other light but important physical labor.

That year, the circus gave me my first stateroom and anybody who ever has traveled with a railroad circus knows that to get a single berth is hard enough; a stateroom is like a citation from Congress.

But I got one and I was mighty happy to have it. I slept in the upper berth and kept it collapsed and out of the way until bedtime. This gave me room enough to sit and read and write, and cook a midnight snack on a little electric unit I put in. A friend in Washington gave me a small icebox; Ernestine Clark and her mother made me some drapes; and I was happy as a lark. One night Merle Evans caught me cooking a couple of ears of corn which I had bought out of season because I was still a farm boy at heart and longed for some roasting ears. By the time I had shucked them, they weren't any bigger than my thumb, but I was cooking them anyhow. The band leader still kids me about my "pigeon-size" roasting ears.

Most show people decorate their walls with circus pictures, but my stateroom has a picture of a farm pond; another of a hayrack and a team of horses. The fellow who first said, "You can take the boy out of the country, but you can't take the country out of the boy," had my number.

In the summer of 1946, I received a letter from Bertram Mills Circus, asking me if I would be interested in returning to the London Olympia for the Christmas show.

I remembered the promise I had made that I would come back for the first post-war circus, and I was anxious to see England and my friends there again. So I sent a letter of acceptance and wrote to Washington for a renewal of pass-

232

port. I booked passage on the *Queen Elizabeth* and sailed from New York in a snowstorm in early December.

We landed late in Southampton. It was cold and damp and the boat train to London did not start on time. When we finally arrived at Waterloo Station, there was a shortage of the wheelbarrow baggage men and not enough taxicabs. Everybody seemed to be sharing cabs, so when my turn came I got in with a young married couple. They hadn't been on the steamship, but claimed part of the cab anyhow and I was glad to get anything for I knew the circus was due to start at 8:15 that very night.

Instead of heading direct for Olympia, the driver took these people to some out-of-the-way part of town to pick up a roll of linoleum. As we drove along, I began to see the first effects of war bombing—flattened areas and some shattered buildings.

We tied the linoleum on top of the cab and I was all the while as nervous as a bridegroom about to be late for his wedding. I certainly wanted to make that circus opening on the dot. We had more trouble getting the linoleum off the top of the taxi before the driver headed for my destination. When I finally landed in the building, the show was ready to start. I went straight to Mr. Mills to report my arrival. He said, "My God! Can you get made up in a hurry? Clement Attlee is in the seats and he is going to stay only for the first fifteen minutes of the show. The newspaper photographers are there waiting to shoot pictures of you with him."

I got my trunk into the dressing room, and I made up faster than ever before in my life. But when I entered the ring, the parliamentary labor leader was gone. The photographers had snapped him, however, and waited then for me. They matched two pictures in the morning edition and ran a caption over all, reading as though a quote from Attlee: "Atta boy, Kelly. Job Well Done."

After I worked through my first routine, I had some time in which to go around and shake hands with the other performers. The warmth of their greeting almost brought tears to my eyes. I really felt at home again with these wholehearted people and I went to work with such high spirits that it was a wonder to me it didn't show beneath the sad makeup "Willie" and I wore in the ring.

I had not had time to buy a loaf of bread or a head of cabbage to use as a familiar prop, so the Manetti brothers went out and got me a loaf of bread. As I made my rounds of the arena with it, I kept wondering what people in the audience meant when they'd say, "Where did you get the 'B. U's'?," until one of the performers told me it meant Bread Units and that bread was rationed.

During intermission, I met with the old gang, the band leader and the ringmaster and some others, at the same old Watney Pub, in the Olympia building. I noticed that the sandwiches were much thinner and that there was very little meat in them. As the show went on, I did what I always had done before—visited the upper balconies where the poorer people sat. After one round up there, I came out with tears in my eyes. Coat sleeves were worn thin or patched; there were runs in the stockings of the girls. All the clothing looked shabby and my mind went back to the more prosperous days in this same place before the terrible war years.

But the thing that touched me most was that these spectators remembered me. They asked me where the head of cabbage was and they still held out their little paper sacks and offered candy to the old hobo clown. I knew that this stuff was rationed. The little children would smile at me and invite me to take a sweet from the sack. Before the war these folks had sat here with boxes of chocolates in their laps. Now there were three or four pitifully tiny pieces in a bag. I hadn't the heart to take even one, so I would reach my fingers into the sack

234

and pretend to take one and pop it into my mouth and eat it as though it was the best piece of candy I ever had. It was amusing to watch the kids peek back into the poke and count the pieces that were left and then say: "Mommie, he didn't take one!"

That London winter left its mark on the record for being one of the coldest in recent memory. I stayed at the Mount Royal, which before the war had been much like the American hotels. But now, when I went home at night after the show, the heat was turned off because of the coal shortage. In the morning, the same well-mannered English waiters would escort me to the breakfast table, but the menu was just fish and sausage (with very little meat in the sausage) and tea or coffee. There also was one slice of bread and a small pat of butter and one lump of sugar. I thought of the big English breakfasts of the pre-war days. Sometimes when I was especially hungry, I would start kicking myself at having left the good old U.S.A. to come over here and starve through a circus contract that I didn't need. Then I would remember that first night at Olympia and the people in the seats who were so much worse off than I was, materially, and I would think about the performers and how they had offered me their ration coupons. Then I thought about the war and the spirit of these wonderful people and I was proud to have them for my friends.

Despite the extremely cold weather, the circus sold out every show. The people seemed to need the circus as much as the circus needed the people and it was a great engagement. The Circus Fans reunion took place and I did a comedy juggling act with dishes, most of which I managed to drop and break. I had no easel for my cartoon act so I drew Bernard Mills' portrait on a white tablecloth which was auctioned off for twenty pounds for a charity.

I visited my favorite markets and found there was little for sale. I made the rounds of Piccadilly and Leicester Square and went out to Saint Paul's Cathedral. One whole square mile flattened out.

I was entitled to a limited ration book for food and clothing. I registered and got my coupons and counted them and discovered I had enough to buy one shirt, which I did not need, so I gave it to one of the boys in the dressing room. The food coupons I never had a chance to use because it was necessary to register with one store and there always was a long line of women with their baskets and I did not have time. I gave my book to an usherette and she got me my allotment —she brought me two eggs.

When the circus engagement was finished, I had two weeks to wait for my sailing. I was lonesome during this time for the circus which had moved out to Ascot. The weather got worse and worse but we finally sailed on schedule, and that sailing day was a great one for me. I missed my English friends, but I was anxious to get a good breakfast of eggs and bacon and to be somewhere that was warm. I had been used to staying in my hotel room a good deal of the time with my overcoat on. Now, in the warmth of my cabin, I shed my coat and in the dining room I nearly ate myself into a stupor.

After getting off the steamship in Manhattan and checking my luggage, I took a slow walk up Broadway. Although I had been away only a few months, it seemed like a long, long time, and I stopped dead in my tracks to see the windows loaded with hams and turkeys, butter and eggs. It sure looked different from London.

Soon, I took a train for Sarasota where the circus was in rehearsal. The sun was out and the weather was hot and my friends were there getting ready for the tour. Except for playing in the British Isles and in Canada, I had not worked outside the States until during the latter part of the 1949 circus tour when rumors began to fly thick and fast about a post-season date in Havana, and Pat Valdo asked me if I wanted to play Cuba.

I asked him if he thought my kind of clowning would go over in Cuba where I'd always understood the people went for the talking variety of circus comedy like Polidor, a long-time favorite there. Pat said he thought they would take to me okay, so I told him I would go along.

We did not take the whole Ringling Brothers and Barnum & Bailey Circus to Havana. At the close of the tour in America, we singled out some of the feature acts, some menagerie animals and props, and left most of the physical part of the big show in winter quarters. We did not need to take tents or seats because the Havana engagement was to be in a building with a general layout similar to the Olympia arena.

Our animals and equipment went by steamer, and most of the people in chartered planes. In Havana, I had almost no rehearsing to do, so I spent most of three days looking over the interesting old city. In some sections, I came upon many people dressed almost as ragged as I was in my hobo costume. The horrible thought struck me that the Cubans might think I was making fun of their poor instead of trying to portray the sad and harmless American "bo."

I peeked through the curtains on opening night, just as I had done that first time in England, anxiously studying my audience. Once, I had feared that the British would be stiff and cold to me. They weren't. Now I wondered if this Spanish-country crowd would be hotheaded and impatient with me. Anyhow, I figured to do my best and soon I'd know one way or the other.

I took a broom and went out into the ring and started sweeping at the little white puddle the spotlight threw at my feet and as I gave the people in the seats my sad stare, I noticed they seemed restless. They soon began stomping their feet and the kids would holler *"Piaso!"* at me and there seemed to be a lot of hissing. It all gathered momentum until I couldn't stand the din and left the ring. I knew "Willie" and I at last had found some people who didn't go for us. We were a flop in Havana. I walked to the back of the building where the show was all lined up and ready to go on. I looked out over the Gulf of Mexico. One hundred and ten miles straight across was Key West, Florida. I wished I was there and that I never had come over to Cuba.

I walked over to Harry Nelson, one of our clowns who speaks Spanish and asked him what they meant by all that stomping. Were they still giving me the razzberry? Harry laughed. "Emmett," he said, "you are too sensitive; the show is fifteen minutes late and they are impatient."

Then I asked him why they yelled *Piaso* at me all the time. "That is their word for clown," he explained, "and they were trying to get your attention."

"Well, answer me this, Harry: why did they keep waving me away from them?"

Nelson laughed and said, "In Cuba, that means they want you to come closer."

I felt better now, but one more thing I wanted to know. "Why did they hiss me?"

Then he really laughed. "That isn't hissing as we know it in America; that's part of the hand waving—to get your attention just as we do it when we yell 'Hey.' "

At this point, the whistle blew and the show started and I worked with a lighter heart the rest of the evening because I knew "Willie" and I had some brand new friends—the Cuban people.

It was warm and I went to the back of the building again at the end of the performance and looked out again toward the Florida coast. The waves looked beautiful this time and everything was different. Well, I thought, the good old U.S.A.

will just have to wait five more weeks for me now. I'm happy here and satisfied.

Business was terrific. We played every day but Monday and it was then I did my shopping and sight-seeing. I spoke no Spanish, but still got along pretty well. The food was good and there were plenty of American newspapers and magazines on the stands. The people of Havana were hospitable and when I boarded a plane to return to Florida, I thought I would like to come back again. Which I did, several times.

One of the biggest thrills of my lifetime came the following autumn. We were up in the Northwest and heading south for California and I was wondering if I ever would get any kind of a break in motion pictures. Almost any actor would like to have some experience in the film medium, but while I had been out in movieland many times nothing had ever happened. I said to "Willie" that if we had got along without a movie contract all these years, we could keep on doing without it.

Our Los Angeles engagement was for several days and our tents were on the big parking lot of the Pan Pacific Auditorium. The first performance was to be for charity, and one hundred ten movie people were to join the circus performers in making it a gala event. Valdo came to me and said that my job was to help figure out clown gags for Van Johnson, Bing Crosby and Frank Sinatra.

This really was some helter-skelter affair, with people running everywhere and the clock-like precision of the big show somewhat disturbed by the problem of working our guest performers into the pattern of things. The movie folks were fine to work with and they loved the atmosphere of the circus back yard. They had their own dressing tent set up and their own makeup artists were on hand.

I rounded up Van Johnson and explained my gag that took place in the riding act. When Justino Loyal, our riding comedian that year, missed his tandem somersault from one galloping horse to another, Johnson was to take a ladder and prop it up against the horse, climb up and sweep off the back of the horse. It went as well as ever.

Bing Crosby was no problem; he was willing and anxious to do anything, and he and I clowned the whole show together. I lost complete track of Frank Sinatra and while I was hunting for him I saw a fellow with my tramp makeup on, waiting to get into the clown car. He yelled at me and asked me if I knew who he was. I didn't. "I'm Frank 'Kelly' Sinatra!" he yelled back.

My friend Hedda Hopper sat on an elephant and pounded her typewriter. Everybody worked hard and everybody had a good time and our "Hollywood opening" was a great success from all angles. Then we headed for Long Beach and I thought to myself: "Well, it happened again. I played Los Angeles and Hollywood and nothing broke for me in the way of a picture deal." As I was brooding about this in the dressing wagon of our juggler, Francis Brunn, a man came up and called to me to come outside. He was Henry Wilson, a motion-picture agent, and he wanted to know if I would be interested in a studio contract with David O. Selznick.

First-off, I told him I figured he would turn out to be like most agents—just a lot of promises, but he insisted he was authorized to make a deal with me. We got together on money and he promised to bring me a contract. My thoughts went immediately to the circus picture which Selznick had said he would make: *The Greatest Show on Earth*. In fact, during our Los Angeles engagement, there had been a big banner hanging inside the top of the menagerie tent, announcing that David O. Selznick would produce in the following year an epic picture called *The Greatest Show on Earth*. DeMille finally produced it instead, but that's another story.

The circus left town and headed east and I had not received any movie contract. We played Phoenix, Arizona, and still no contract. In Tucson, on the worst lot of the season, with dust blowing everywhere, there stood my agent—dressed to kill and with a bundle under his arm. We went to his hotel room and he read me the contract word for word. Selznick wanted to tie up my services for a year, which meant I could not troupe with the circus.

I went to Pat Valdo and explained that I had a fine offer for film work. He wanted to know how much and I told him. It was much more than I received with the circus. "Well," said the circus personnel boss, "I'll be glad to see you get it. We'll miss you, Emmett, but that kind of money will buy a lot of green onions and I know how well you like green onions."

I was upset because one clause of my movie contract specified that the film company would break the first publicity story. This meant that I couldn't tell my friends on the circus what I was going to do. Soon, however, on the day we played San Antonio, Texas, I walked onto the show grounds and several people asked me if I had read Louella Parsons' column in which she had written, "What is David O. Selznick going to do with the sad-faced clown who eats cabbage?"

The circus closed its tour at the winter quarters city of Sarasota and I went to the West coast to start my work in pictures. I had an appointment to meet Selznick and went there with my agent. The film genius was walking around in his stocking feet, his coat off, apparently deep in thought as to what he was going to do with me.

We discussed several ideas, but this was a new field to me and I figured I had better let Selznick and the agent do most of the talking. Selznick struck me as one of the most intelligent men I had ever talked with, but I left the studio without the faintest idea of what I was to do. Every Friday, at the Roosevelt Hotel where I lived in Hollywood, my check was in the box although almost nothing was required of me.

This was a new kind of show business to me. I was accustomed to playing twice a day, rain or shine, and not being paid to do nothing. I kept in touch with the studio publicity department, however, and we did a few stunts, one was with an elephant out at the Burbank Airport. The elephant was supposed to remember me from years ago. I never had seen the elephant before and I doubt if the elephant ever had seen me.

Another stunt was for the March of Dimes and another was a hospital show for children. These things I always am happy to do. Then there was a stunt to publicize the premiere of a Clark Gable picture. I was in tramp costume and wore a big badge that said, VISITING MAYOR FROM SARASOTA, FLORIDA.

There were twenty-two cameras clicking away and the stunt turned out just fine for me, but I kept wondering when I was going to go to work in a picture. The money they were paying me wasn't hay and I reckoned they'd not go on doing it forever.

By this time, Selznick's interest in making *The Greatest Show on Earth* had been taken over by DeMille. Columnists wrote that I was to be in that circus picture, but I had heard nothing official about it. I was restless and I missed the circus, so I asked my agent if he thought I could arrange to fly to Chicago and visit the show. He fixed it up, but he cautioned me to be handy to a telephone. "If Selznick calls for you, I want you here at once!"

I took a room in the Stevens Hotel (now the Hilton) in Chicago, overlooking the Illinois Central tracks where the circus would be coming in. I was like a country kid again, up early and waiting to see the show come to town. I even had binoculars. When I saw the circus train's first section rolling in, a great wave of homesickness hit me. I hurried over to the grounds and had a great day of reunion with my pals.

242

It commenced to rain and the next day it rained again and the third day it rained even harder. I didn't care; I was "home" again and happy.

I had planned to stay the whole week, but on the third day there was a note in my hotel mailbox from my agent. It told me that I would have to fly back to the West coast at once. I was cast in a film with Jack Smart and it was to be called *The Fat Man*.

> You can shake the sawdust out of your shoes,
> but you can't shake it out of your heart.
>
> *Cecil B. DeMille*

MAGIC LANTERNS

In *The Fat Man,* a title taken from a successful radio serial that featured Jack Scott Smart, a large, affable and talented actor of stage, screen and radio, I was cast as the "heavy," which is what the theatre calls the villain. They gave me a manuscript to take home with me and study, and I was thrilled pink.

But not for long. The farther I got into that manuscript, the more depressed I became. The story called for me to kill a dentist, then a nurse, and to top it off, I was to burn a fellow in a truck. Then I was to take a wad of ill-gotten money and start my own circus and hide there behind the makeup of a clown. I was to be discovered when they saw me without the makeup. Naturally they wanted my hobo clown disguise and they tested me this way the next day.

I tested all right for the cameras, but I was sick at heart. I wondered what children in the circus tent would think of me when they'd remember me as the killer in a movie they'd seen. It worried me so much I couldn't sleep. Saturday night, I went to a spot called Christine's Cafe which some friends I'd made in movieland frequented. I talked with Walt Disney

245

and he was cool on the idea of a well-known circus comic being cast in a film as a killer. People are inclined to accept a movie actor in the parts they have watched him do on the screen. You can be the sweetest guy in the world and if the public sees you do somebody dirt on celluloid, that's the way they add you up; you can be a first-class, no-good heel, but if you are a hero in a picture, you'll be a hero to the people who see it—at least until they meet you in person and make up their minds for themselves about you as a person.

A Warner producer named Foy told me not to worry; it was just a matter of acting. I received as many opinions as the number of persons whose opinion I asked.

There were two paintings hung back of the bar. One was of the whiteface clown, Felix Adler; the other was of me. A fellow whose name I never caught and who was a little inebriated had listened to me talk about my problem. He kept pointing to my picture and saying, "Don't let *him* do the killing! No, no; not *him!* Let the other fellow do it."

Right then and there I got an idea. I would switch my makeup!

I called my agent the next day and he didn't like the idea at all. He told me that this was no time to start revising; that they were going to begin shooting the picture in a few days. I told him to get hold of Selznick for a conference. This he did not want to do until I insisted I was ready to break my contract if I had to commit those murders made up in my traditional hobo character.

It was arranged for me to talk with Producer Aubrey Schenck and Director Bill Castle. Neither of them gave me any encouragement. I was at the point of desperation as I sat in that plush office. "Willie" seemed to keep pleading with me. He was lying in my trunk up in the Roosevelt Hotel, and while it may seem that all there was to "Willie" was a threadbare suit and a putty nose and some grease paint and a busted derby and a pair of big, flapping shoes, I knew that "Willie" had a heart, too. We were one and the same and I felt I'd be a heel if I sold him out and made a real bum of him even in this crazy land of make-believe.

"Willie" seemed to say: "Emmett, don't do this to me! I am a tramp, but I'm not a bad guy and I don't want to harm anybody. Good tramps don't harm anybody. And I love children. Don't do it!"

Well, just when it looked as if I was in a jam I never could get out of, Jack Smart came to my rescue. "Gentlemen," he said, "I am an actor and I can see Kelly's point of view. Let him wear some makeup other than his hobo clown."

The director reluctantly let me suggest another makeup and so my meager ability as an artist backed me up. I drew five separate clown faces right there in the office and asked them if I could make up like one of them for this part of a murderer. The one they picked was the makeup I had worn as a whiteface clown in the circus prior to the time when I had switched to "Willie," the hobo.

"Okay," the director said. "Let's see what it looks like."

I could see he was skeptical. Anyhow, on Monday, I took my stuff to the studio with me and carefully made up in whiteface. It was a chalk-talk comic I created, tear streaks painted from the eyes; tight skullcap, red tufts of hair over the ears, cone-style cap; striped shirt and loose pants and big shoes. I walked onto the set and the director said, "I didn't think you could do it."

The only thing I had to change was the mouth; he wanted it more wistful—like the hobo character's. I changed that and we started the picture the next morning.

I found that the movie schedule was something I would have to get used to. It was tough to get up so early. I had to report in makeup on the lot by eight o'clock in the morning and be on the set by nine. I did my own clown makeup, but

247

the studio made me up for the straight part in the earlier sequences of the film.

I sat around doing nothing until noon when they called me for the first scene, which was the murder of the dentist. I was to go down a long, wide walk and through a glass door and into a hotel bedroom where I was to clout the man over the head with a rubber revolver.

I never had done anything like that and so this was a scene I couldn't seem to get the feel of. That's where the director had to step in and show me how to grab the man by the collar and be vicious. We took that scene seven times before I finally got it. The man was an old character actor and he was such a pleasant person it was tough for me to get used to "killing" him and dragging him to a window where I'd toss him out to fall sixteen floors. Of course, when I pushed him through the window, he fell only a few feet onto a mattress.

The director and everyone else was very kind to me because they realized I was used to working to an audience and accustomed to getting immediate reaction from spectators and that this was different. All I could see was bright lights and the shadowy people standing in the back of the set and it was all strange. But after the first day I began to get the feel of it.

We worked until six o'clock that evening. Next morning I saw the rushes which had been developed the night before and it felt strange to see myself walking around on the screen in a double-breasted suit, black hat, gloves and a slick haircut instead of in my old, ragged tramp outfit. Naturally, they had needed to make me menacing and I hadn't realized that I could look so cussed mean.

We worked for three weeks on this picture. In the latter sequences, they set up a circus setting—tent and ticket wagon and all the trimmings and I began to feel almost at home. In one scene, I was to fall from the top of the tent into a net. All I did was fall forward onto a pile of mattresses in a close-up. I wanted to do the real thing and could have done it easily, but because of the insurance restrictions the studio didn't want me to take a chance.

The pay-off on all this precaution was that I broke a rib just jumping off a low bandstand with a gun in my hand. I stubbed my toe when I fell and hit the ground hard and blanked out. When I came to, they asked me if I was hurt and I felt foolish and said no. That night, I couldn't sleep for a pain in my chest and next morning discovered I had cracked a rib in falling against the revolver.

Jane Meadows played the part of the nurse and it was up to me to choke her. I hated this scene because she was such a nice person and she had to scream while I did the dirty work.

I was going by the lunchroom on the day they first set up the circus scene. Someone called to me and said, "Emmett, this is *your* circus." In the story, I was Mr. Deets and the lettering on the circus wagons proclaimed that this was Ed. Deets' show. I became fond of this little make-believe circus— so much so that when the shooting was over and the set was dismantled, I felt the same old lonely sensation that one gets when the circus is gone and there is nothing left but the sod and the trees and a few empty peanut sacks. "Ed. Deets' Circus" had left town.

When we finished the shooting on schedule and when I saw the pieces fitted together into a complete story, it was an entirely new kind of thrill. The scene at the finish where I lay bleeding and dying made me feel squeamish even though it was only on the screen.

My contract wasn't renewed by Selznick, so I had my agent call Cecil B. DeMille who was in Sarasota for the initial filming of *The Greatest Show on Earth*. I didn't want to miss being in what gave promise of being the biggest circus film of all time. From California I had telephoned the circus and had made arrangements to come back for the tour. After a brief visit with some of my family in Indiana, I went to New York City and the Madison Square Garden opening of the big show. It felt good to see the freshly painted red and gold wagons rolling into the building. Seeing the old gang was even more wonderful. Most of their talk was about the filming that DeMille had done in circus winter quarters.

The circus opened as usual and I was back into the swing of it when DeMille's production manager, Roy Burns, came to see me about being in the picture. We came to terms and the circus gave me a release so that the movie people could shoot some of my scenes in California. Meanwhile, I continued to appear with the circus, but one morning I received a hurry-up call and a few hours and one fast plane trip later I landed on the Paramount lot and was ready to go to work in the picture.

The first day there, I went to what is called New York Street. They were all ready for DeMille to come onto the set. While we were waiting there, I looked over the big scene of the circus train wreck. It was mighty realistic, and almost seemed as though some of our real Pullman cars were turned over.

Promptly at nine o'clock Cecil DeMille walked onto the set with his famous leather boots and pleasant smile. He shook my hand and made me feel right at home. Then we went over some of the scenes I was to be in. This picture was much bigger in scope than my other film, and this time I was relieved to learn that "Willie" and I would just be ourselves and that I would not have any lines to speak. I am essentially a circus clown and a pantomimist and lines worry me. This time I did not have to study lines at night and lie awake worrying about making a mistake in front of the camera next morning.

Eventually, however, I did have one line. There were two words in it. It occurred in the wreck scene where Betty Hutton asked me to get the clowns ready to give a parade. My big speech consisted of "What? Parade?" And it took two shots to do even that.

Jimmy Stewart and I worked in several scenes together and these were later matched with authentic circus backgrounds that had been shot in Sarasota or on the road with the show. I got a great kick out of one scene in which I was sitting on a wagon and playing solitaire when the wind blew the cards away. This was accomplished with an air hose. Like several other scenes destined to be matched or dubbed into previously taken shots, this one was filmed against a yellow screen. When matched up and ready for use in the film, I was in a street parade on Sarasota's main street with crowds waving and stores passing slowly by.

One morning, during the filming on the Paramount lot, I was surprised to see my boss, John Ringling North, dressed in riding boots and made up for work in the film. I wasn't on call that day, so I sauntered over to watch the shooting and I thought Johnny did very well.

The circus was finishing its Boston engagement now and soon would open under canvas in Washington where a lot more filming would be done. We were notified that we'd fly to join the circus there. At daybreak, a lot of cameras and other heavy equipment were loaded into the plane I was to ride. I looked at that mass of heavy stuff and began to wish they had sent me by train. But it was an uneventful flight with only one stop en route, at Chicago.

Never did the big show look prettier than when we spotted it from the sky. Flags flying on new, colored canvas and brightly painted wagons spotted around surely made a lovely sight for "Willie" and me.

I was a little embarrassed and in a sort of a spot because I was with the circus and still in a way I was not with it. I was contracted to Paramount and they put me up in the Mayflower Hotel and provided limousines to take us to the lot. I felt a little foolish stepping out of these limousines at the circus back yard, for I was afraid my friends would think I was putting on the dog. I explained to them that it was just part of the deal and they laughed and said not to feel that way at all —that I wasn't the first "bum" who'd ever ridden in a limousine. So I felt all right after that, but I was careful to stay a circus man at heart and not start getting stars in my eyes.

We kept the same hours on this job that we'd kept on the Paramount lot, which meant that we hit the show grounds at eight o'clock in the morning. I wasn't used to it in my circus surroundings where I never came around before noon in preparation for a matinee that began at 2:15.

I did a scene with Dorothy Lamour and Jimmy Stewart right there on the circus, but the rest of my stuff was shot in the studio. The movie crew and actors and DeMille and the others moved with the circus to Philadelphia and did some more shooting and then flew back to California. I was hoping I could stay with the circus now, but instead I received orders to be ready at the airport with the rest of the movie crowd. The picture was finished on the West coast and after a total of fifteen weeks my Paramount contract was up. By that time the circus was out in the Middle West and the question arose as to which town I'd join in. Valdo said it would be all right for me to come back in Denver, so the studio paid my transportation back to the show and I was soon on my way to being a circus man again.

I arrived in Denver on Friday and the circus wasn't due in town until Sunday night—for a Monday exhibition. I wandered around town, looking at the circus posters, and finally went into the *Denver Post* to see if there was anybody there I knew. The show's advance reserved seat ticket sale was going on and I chatted with our ticket man, Harry Burt. Just then the paper's feature editor happened along and nabbed me for a stunt. This was a Sunday baseball game between newspapermen and radio men. I was to go in as a pinch hitter and wear my hobo outfit and makeup.

I had my "wardrobe" and makeup with me in the hotel, so I agreed to do it. The publicity, I figured, might help the circus engagement on Monday if it hit the street in the noontime edition of the *Post* on circus day. This paper always has been friendly to circuses because it once was owned by Fred Bonfils and Harry Tammen who numbered the famous Sells-Floto Circus among their holdings. Helen Bonfils, well-known theatrical producer, actress and Denver philanthropist, is one of the principal stockholders of the *Post* today and she likes circus people, as does Palmer Hoyt, her editor.

My Sunday luck was against me. It was the hottest day of the year and I had on my full regalia. When I got out on the diamond, I discovered that they were playing for keeps. This was hard ball and I hadn't played since I was a kid. I nearly threw my shoulder out of place trying to connect with that baseball. I missed the first pitch, and the second. I let two balls go by. Then I started to burn. I wanted to hit that ball more than anything I'd ever wanted in my life. Maybe the pitcher felt sorry for me and threw over an easy one; anyhow I slammed it over the shortstop's head and out into left field.

The problem then was to make it to first base on my flapping clown shoes before they threw me out. I just made it, all out of wind, and they really were playing for keeps. They put in a pinch runner after the camera men got the pictures and I was free to go back to town and cool off.

Monday, I went out to the show grounds to rejoin the big show. The tents, which I'd seen bright and shining in Washington, D.C., at the start of the tour, now were showing the wear and tear of the tour, but it was home to me. When I went to the dressing tent, Otto Griebling was all excited. He told me how, in Cheyenne, Wyoming, on Saturday, he had arranged with the manager of a movie theatre to run a special

253

midnight showing of *The Fat Man,* and that almost the whole circus had gone up to see it. He wasn't kidding. As I made the rounds to greet my friends after an absence of more than three months, I found that all they wanted to talk about was *The Fat Man.*

The circus headed into the Northwest and then went down the Pacific coast and into California where there was a big reunion of the DeMille-Paramount crowd with the circus folks who had helped make *The Greatest Show on Earth.* Here, there was some disappointment, for a lot of our gang had expected to see a preview of the film they'd worked in. But DeMille said he preferred to wait until the picture was completely put together. I did see quite a bit of it, piece by piece, and without sound, in the studio, but I knew I wouldn't know what we really had until I could see it complete.

The circus tour closed in Florida in late November. *The Greatest Show on Earth* had opened at Radio City in New York and all the reviews were raves. Now, the road premiere was to take place in Sarasota, the home of the "Big One."

The town was really in a stir. There was to be a night parade and I was to be in it, although they hadn't told me what I was to do. Somebody told me that I was to ride with the mayor in an open car and that sounded all right to "Willie" and me. But when Valdo finally gave me my instructions, he said, "You do not ride with the mayor; you ride with the governor of the State of Florida."

In the parade through the lamp-lit streets to the Florida Theatre there were the high-school band and other local units, and the circus had contributed some cages and walking animals. We all wound up at the front of the theatre which was decorated to resemble the main entrance of a circus. There were cameras flashing and some words at a microphone and then we all went inside.

There were a lot of preliminary speeches and coast-to-

coast telephonic conversation with DeMille and remarks by
city officials. I was not called upon and I was glad of it; I am
not good at that sort of thing. At last the picture we had made
in so many locations and over quite a long period of time
started to unfold and as I watched it, I was both thrilled and
proud to be in it. I sent Cecil DeMille a telegram of congratu-
lation that night. He is a man with a true feel for the circus;
he respects it and he made a great picture.

When the circus tour started the following spring, I was
curious to get the reaction of people from town to town who
had seen the film. There was an agreement between Paramount and the circus that the movie would not be shown day-
and-date, but would come to town either before or after the
circus engagement.

Sometimes what happens off the record in the filming of
a thriller is more exciting than what the public sees on the
screen. Such an occasion was the day when it came time for
a circus aerialist named Joe Alexander to double for the movie
actor, Cornel Wilde, in a fall from a trapeze rigging to the
ground. A large hole had been dug in the ground and a flying-
act net spread over it. This was covered with reeds to conceal
it. The camera was to catch the fall and record the actual
hitting of what looked to be the ground when the actor came
crashing to earth.

Concello, the circus general manager and former flying-
trapeze champ, looked over the set-up and shook his head. It
looked risky; it was a very long drop. To make sure the stunt
was safe for Alexander, he took one fall himself. The hole
had half-filled with water during the night because the scene
was filmed at circus winter quarters and you don't dig very
deep at Sarasota without getting sea water. Concello hit the
net and went right on through.

A circus is a bright, spangled girl with a date in a town a hundred miles away tomorrow morning.

THE ALLEY

I never think of clown alley during the hectic days of World War II without getting a mental flash-back of Paul Jerome and his double-duty routine.

Jerome clowned in the circus performance and helped the customers get their minds off the war for a while, but back in the dressing tent he reversed his field and kept reminding us of the stark nature of the world outside. He was Uncle Sam's self-appointed pitchman for war stamps and savings bonds and he was good at it, too. Several times a week he would feel the urge to climb up on his trunk and deliver a patriotic talk for the "Uncle."

This usually happened when Paul was less than half dressed, and one afternoon a visiting newspaperman remarked about both the amount of money the clown raised and the informality of his public speaking costume. "Hell!" said Jerome, "who cares about clothes? This is a national emergency!"

Emergencies are nothing new to the joeys, but not many ever had to meet one like Paul Horompo did one afternoon when the circus was in Madison Square Garden for its spring engagement. Horompo is a midget and he was dressed as one of the seven dwarfs in a "Snow White" walk-around which came early in the performance. Standing in the corridor that led from the Garden's "backstage" to the "front of the house," or main lobby, he was waiting quietly all alone—because he had dressed early and the other clowns weren't there yet—when a tiger came streaking through the hall like a bolt of orange lightning.

"Lady" had escaped in the back of the building, slashed a donkey that was lined up for the grand entry, wheeled away from the menagerie men who had come to capture her and headed through that corridor.

It opened into the main lobby where the public still was milling around and the place was full of children. If the tiger ever had got that far, there is no telling what might have happened. Horompo added up all these things very quickly in his mind. Instead of running for his life, he stood straight in the path of the big cat and hit her over the head with a little papier-mâché pick such as he and the other dwarfs carried in the walk-around.

Needless to say the prop pick didn't hurt the tiger or even stun her, but it must have surprised her a lot, for in her confusion she spun around and headed the other way— straight into a net that the animal men dropped over her. The rest was easy. Nobody in the crowd that afternoon realized that "Dopey" had been anything but just that a few minutes before he came marching around the hippodrome track to the merry tune of "Heigh ho, heigh ho; it's off to work we go."

But word of Paul's courage and quick thinking reached the papers and the radio stations, so that a week later a big network show called "We, the People" flew our Dopey back to New York from the Boston engagement to be the hero of the broadcast.

To the men who have the alley as a business address,

something unexpected is always happening, and a lot of it is pure, cussed misery—especially in hard rainstorms when water runs through the dressing tent like a small river and forces us to put our trunks up on tent stakes laid flat on the ground. Still and all, I must admit that every once in a while some unlooked-for event turns into a real dividend and we stumble right into the richest find that a clown could ask for—an unexpected laugh.

It happened to Felix Adler on an afternoon when he was late because he had gone uptown to do a broadcast and his cab driver got into a traffic jam while trying to hurry Felix back to the show grounds. By the time he hit the lot the clowns were all lined up for their first entrance. Adler ran for the dressing top, pulled on a costume, grabbed his wig and high-tailed it for the big top.

This time, he got giggles not only from the audience; the other clowns laughed, too. Felix had a bad moment or so while he wondered if he might have forgotten his pants, but what brought the guffaws was the fact that he had been in such a hurry he had forgotten to put on his makeup. A clown dressed for the ring but with his own face in plain view was pretty funny. There wasn't any future in it, however, and Felix reverted to type as soon as he could get back to the alley.

Adler got another unexpected laugh one time when he was dressed as the big bad wolf and had trained three small pigs to follow him around the track. A piece of rigging fell from the top of the tent, conked the clown on the head and knocked him cold. When he came to, in a few seconds, he was lying flat on his back and the pigs were all over him, licking his face. The crowd loved it and I guess that more than half of them probably thought it was all part of the act.

Another time, there was a circus act that required a tank of water. A clown, running pell-mell around the hippodrome track, stumbled into it and came out soaking wet—his neat, starched white suit looking as if it had been through the wringer.

Well, the crowd just leaned back and roared at this one and, unluckily for the clown, the circus manager happened to be in the big top and the upshot was that he decided to have the poor joey do it at every performance.

Many clown costumes are real works of art. They aren't the carelessly made stuff you'd rent from a commercial costume house for a Halloween party or a Mardi gras. And a circus person can always tell if a clown is a professional by such things as the cut of the ruffled collar and the cuffs. Shoes and wigs are another tip-off as to the experience and general know-how in a clown. A wig from which the hair stands straight up (usually red) is called a fright wig. Quite a few joeys are clever with needle and thread and can make their own costumes; others have their suits made to specification by women in the circus wardrobe department.

Makeups are many and while it may seem to the average spectator that all clowns look alike, they really don't. Once a joey invents an original way of making up his face, he gets a sort of moral copyright or gentlemen's agreement on it and nobody else copies it exactly. As my "Willie" started to gain prominence, several clowns on other circuses copied my appearance and some of my gags, and one of these jokers got me into no end of trouble because he did an unprofessional thing at an indoor circus in Washington, D.C. and got his picture into the papers while doing it. He sat in the lap of a nationally prominent woman and while the crowd laughed, the woman naturally was embarrassed. A lot of people saw the picture and the guy looked just enough like me to make people think Emmett Kelly committed this breach of professional etiquette.

In contrast to my hobo routines, the rule in most circus

clowning is that the spectator must be surprised and surprised in a hurry. Clowns in the modern circus arena are simply a few bright moments in a fast-moving razzle dazzle of spinning acrobats, prancing horses, flying-trapeze artists and the like. What is known as a clown "stop" is a brief appearance of the joeys while props are being set for a ring or an aerial display and we are supposed to do our stuff and get out. So the clown gags take place so fast and so often that most of the spectators can't remember when the show is over what it was they laughed at.

One of the fundamentals of clowning is to start out doing something that looks serious and then have it pay off in a ridiculous manner. An example of this is the clown who saws another clown in half. When the saw has gone through the body, each half runs away—each half, in this case, consisting of one dwarf.

Paul Jung is a master at dreaming up elaborate clown numbers and one of his best is the "Reducing Machine." A large man gets into a big box that looks like a steam bath and Jung "turns on the heat." Smoke comes out of the box and so does the man—only now he is less than three feet high. The large man has disappeared into the box and a midget identically dressed has been released through a little door at the side.

Clowns try to make some of their routines as topical as possible. Jung now has a rocket gun that gets a lot of laughs. He loads a dwarf clown into the mouth of the gun and they set it off with a light charge of powder. A dummy clown goes sailing out straight for the top of the building when we do it in Madison Garden; then the spotlight finds a real dwarf clown, similarly dressed, running along one of the aisles as though he had just landed there. The way this one takes place under canvas is to load in the dwarf, who escapes through the end of the cannon, set off the charge and point to the

261

top of the tent where a dummy clown and a parachute are released to come drifting down.

Paul's best, I think, was the "Adam" Smasher and he used it when the atom-bomb publicity was in all the papers and everybody had started talking about atomic research. A goofy-looking clown with a sign on him that read "ADAM" was coaxed into a big, square machine. Only his head stuck out. Other clowns cranked wheels and made adjustments on an instrument dial and then a padded thing like a pile driver dropped onto his head. He disappeared into the machine and doors flew open on all sides of the box. Through these doors ran midgets all dressed as "Adam" had been dressed when he had gone into the machine. The way the four midget editions of the big clown ran in all directions brought one of the biggest laughs I ever heard in a circus tent.

Jung built a steam roller one year and the gag was for it to run over a clown who got in its path. As it rolled on, this man had disappeared up inside it and on the hippodrome track in its wake was a perfectly flat, oilcloth copy of the "victim." The clowns picked it up tenderly, put it on a stretcher and walked out.

Paul is what circuses call a "producing" clown. This means that instead of working alone, he employs many other clowns for his routines and each is a little production in itself. In a workshop in Tampa, Florida, not far from circus winter quarters, Paul and his pretty wife, Elsie, and half a dozen dwarfs and midgets build the stuff they'll be using in new clown routines. They do beautifully realistic Disney characters, too, for walk-arounds to remind the kids of Dumbo, Pinocchio, the Three Little Pigs, the Seven Dwarfs and others as fast as Disney makes them popular on film.

Most of us use props of one kind or another. Mine aren't very elaborate—an old broom, some lumber, a saw, a head of cabbage, etc., but Lou Jacobs built a tiny car that runs by itself and carries him in it. Jacobs is a big, strapping fellow and how he contorts himself into a car not much bigger than an office-size wastebasket is a kind of minor miracle. There is a howl all over the big top when he emerges from this baby edition of a coupe that has run out into the ring on its own power.

Lou is also a real master of clown makeup and his wardrobe is great. One of the funny things he does is carry a giant-size prop bun with a live dachshund in it to resemble a "hot dog" sandwich.

Quite a few clowns keep pets and train them for the show. Harry Dan has a goose and Frankie Saluto a big rabbit and Charlie Bell has a little fox terrier that he dresses to look like a rabbit. Then Charlie goes "hunting" with a funny-looking old shotgun. He can't find the rabbit—because it always is at his heels. Finally it stays behind and the clown turns around and sees it, and acts scared stiff. He takes aim and a small report comes from the gun and the little "rabbit" falls over and lies still. Charlie picks it up and it is limp as a rag. He drops it into his game bag and walks away. But the bag has no bottom in it and soon the "rabbit" is running along behind the hunter just as happy as you please.

Felix Adler says he has put more "hams" into show business than Rodgers and Hammerstein, Leland Hayward and the Shuberts combined. In point of fact, a pet pig is his trademark and instead of keeping it until it grows up, he trades it in for another little one. He has friends all over the country who select prize porkers for Felix to audition and he then leaves in exchange the one he has trained and which is now too big. Felix trains his "hams" to climb a slide and scoot down. After this, they get a pull on a baby bottle with a nipple.

Paul Jerome gets some of his best effects electrically. He has himself wired from head to foot, but inside his clothes and cleverly concealed. His nose lights up from time to time and he wears a neon heart that flutters in bright red light when he spots a pretty girl in the grandstand. Other joeys get themselves rigged up with water bags to create an artificial rainstorm pouring down on their umbrella or to squirt streams of it from their eyes after somebody has hurt their feelings.

Paul Wentzel has "break-away" britches: his costume is made so that it will unsnap and go flying through the air when pulled by an invisible wire in the hands of some other joey, and by now he has probably lost his pants in public in half the towns of this country. This clown, like Jung, is a real craftsman and builds a great many effects for the production numbers. One year he made wings for the elephants and another time he made clown masques for some of them.

There always is a laugh somewhere from the off-stage antics of the midgets and dwarfs. In a west Texas city a few years ago, Felix Adler and his dwarf pal, Frankie Saluto, had been to a party given by local members of the Circus Fans Association. The festivities ran late and the show trains left on time. When the cab carrying Felix and little Frankie pulled up to the railroad yards, the last section of the show trains had started to move. Felix picked up the dwarf and ran with him in his arms, but their sleeping car had already moved too far for him to make it on foot with his pal in his arms.

Felix did the next best thing; he tossed Frankie onto the observation platform of the last car and raced down the track and caught his own sleeper in the nick of time. On a circus train, many of the cars are dead-end which means that you can't walk through the train from one car to another. That's why Felix couldn't jump on the last car with the dwarf and go on down through the moving train to the car where his bunk was.

The last car happened to be the circus president's private car. Saluto got cold standing on the platform and finally knocked on the door. The show's top boss came and opened it, wearing his pajamas. He saw that the clown was stranded and he invited him inside. A few miles farther on, the train stopped for a few moments and Frankie decided he would get off and run down the tracks to his own sleeper. Usually, when a circus train stops in the night it will stand still for several minutes, awaiting a clear signal. But this time, the train started almost immediately and before Frankie could get back on.

He stood in the middle of the tracks, waving his arms and shouting. In the dim light from the end car, a brakeman saw him and nearly fainted. The dwarf clown was so short that the railroad man thought the train had run over somebody and cut off his legs. He pulled the emergency cord and the train stopped so suddenly it tumbled performers in the aisles and also jammed some of the train's brakes so that there was a matter of several hundred dollars for repairs.

It all made for so much trouble that not until sometime later did the principal players in this little drama realize the humor of the whole thing.

A few of the things that people always ask clowns is if they are happy, how long it takes them to make up their faces, and what they do in their spare time. I can make up my face in five minutes if I have to, but I like to take from twenty minutes to half an hour. We all use mirrors, but after applying the same design for years and years, I guess we could do it blind if we had to. Zinc oxide and glycerine is the base for clown makeup as it is for cold cream and Adler insists that we get a "beauty treatment" whenever we make up our faces. And that we need it.

In our spare time, we sit around the dressing tents and wagons and try to relax. There usually is a checker game going or a few hands of gin rummy. The top lid of the trunk makes a fair writing desk. Our "memory books" are the inside

265

of the trunk top where you'll find a display of family pictures, old route cards and programs. Traditionally, the circus post-man is always a clown. This is a big job and worth the tips the mail carrier receives from the performers at the end of the tour. He'll handle over a thousand individual pieces of mail every day, buy money orders, carry packages and magazines —and get himself some valuable souvenirs if he is a stamp collector, for circus mail comes from all over the world.

Usually, a circus will have several softball teams that play among themselves or occasionally take on a town team. The most fun we ever had with baseball was when there was a team of midgets playing regularly against a girl team. It was a close race to the finish for the several years we ran this "midget world series" and it was a laugh riot all the way.

The best all-around clowns know comedy, music and acrobatics. Some of the older men in the alley are former aerialists, acrobats or equestrians who have been injured and forced to give up their chosen work or, finally, got so much age on them they couldn't "cut it" any longer. But they love the circus and would rather do routine clowning than leave the show.

The "alley" has some fairly well-known alumni like Fred Stone and Red Skelton and a couple of popular clowns with the Ringling show before my time there. One was a short, stocky fellow who wore a baggy moth-eaten fur coat and amused people by blowing smoke into his shirt front, after which it would pour out from under the hem of the long coat. He had a rubber tube that ran through the lining of the coat and this made the trick possible. His partner, a smaller man, wore shell-rim spectacles, and one day when he had mislaid them he simply painted the glasses onto his face with a stick of black grease. This gave him an even greater owl-like look and made a hit with the crowd. He never wore his real glasses for clowning again. They still make folks laugh when he romps through a musical stage show where the name of Bobby Clark is at the top of the comedy heap. His partner, now dead many years, was Paul McCullough.

Clark and McCullough were a team of acrobatic clowns from Springfield, Ohio, where Gus Sun's booking agency guided their steps in their starting period. They went from street-fair jobs to regular circus work and then into burlesque and finally made the grade as stars of the legitimate stage. Like Fred Stone and other stage comedians whose background was circus clowning, Clark and McCullough always used a good many funny props.

But Bobby Clark was an acrobat even before he teamed up with McCullough. His first professional engagement was for an Elks circus presented on the streets of Delaware, Ohio, in the early part of the century. Bobby and his acrobatic teammate were broke and could not afford a hotel, but the man who owned the flying-trapeze act kindly left the net up overnight so the young comedians could sleep in it. The net was so tight that it was scarcely more comfortable than a waffle iron and the pattern of the ropes was clearly seen on Bobby's back next day. The leaper in the flying-trapeze act on that occasion was a talented kid with a ready smile and plenty to smile with. His name was Joe E. Brown.

Some clowns aren't amusing except when they are working in the performance. Others are naturally dead-pan and seldom wear any smile except the one they've painted on, but nearly all are good-humored and we all get along pretty well. In a circus, you mostly have to work so hard that there is little time for fighting anything except time and space and the weather.

There is a story to show how a circus clown's sense of humor didn't let him down even though he was headed straight for the "Big Lot," which is what circus people call Heaven.

Johnny Patterson was his name and he lay dying in the

dressing tent. A town doctor came and looked him over and got ready to leave. "Good night, Mr. Patterson," he said. "I'll see you in the morning."

"I know you will, doc," replied Johnny, "but will I see you?"

Show business has its drawbacks, for the performer especially. He can be good and still be out of work or, as we say, "at liberty," and everyone dreads the in-between-jobs periods when we can't get work.

Even so, the circus performer has it better than the stage actor, for while we may not get as much money, we do receive our board and lodging and we have a seven- or eight-month season. We know that unless there is some disaster to take us off the road, we will play out that much time every year.

There is a bright side to show business, though, and this is it: you can keep at it as long as you are able to work. It isn't like the ordinary business employee's problem when he tries to change his work after the age of fifty. There's a good chance he'll wind up running an elevator or being a night watchman no matter what he has been trained to do. This country is a young-feeling country. We worship youth and we push the youngsters ahead. I'm all for that, but it's rough on a lot of healthy, intelligent older people who could be productive for many years after the usual age of retirement.

But, as I say, show business is a business where you can grow old and keep at it. An acrobat who gets hurt or has too many years on him to keep up the physical grind can shift to easier work. He can clown if he has any talent for it and there are other departments of the circus he can work in. In the theatre, an aging person can shift to character roles. Either place, unless you're a star, you may not draw down the pay envelope you once did, but you'll make a living and you'll still be in the business you love.

268

Frank McClosky, the present general manager of the Ringling Brothers and Barnum & Bailey Circus, and I have a theory that outdoor show business, in spite of its rough-and-tumble, helps keep a person looking young. Speaking of youthful showmen on the shady side of sixty, I'd like to be as jaunty as Frank Braden, one of our press agents, when I'm his age. It was he who worked up the stunt where one of the Ringling midgets sat in the lap of dignified J. Pierpont Morgan during a senatorial investigation in 1933 and caused a publicity sensation. It was credited to various absent agents, but Braden was the only circus press agent in Washington then and it was his stunt.

"Willie" and I have traveled a long, long way together since that day when he was born on my drawing board in Kansas City. A whole lot of it has been done on foot—tramping thousands of miles around the oval of the circus hippodrome, over and over again, nine to fifteen times each show, twice a day rain or shine for the eight months of the tour plus more of the same at the winter indoor circus dates.

The laughter of children is a sound no circus clown ever can forget. It sticks in his mind and he can still hear the echo warming his heart when he has put aside the makeup and the motley and quit trouping.

Once, during World War II, a radio program was being prepared to send to service people overseas and it was to contain the familiar, well-remembered sounds of home—the excitement of the football stadium, the baseball park, the theatre, the voices of church choirs and the like. The circus was asked to contribute something, and so our publicity department came up with the idea that we would record a few minutes of a morning matinee in Madison Square Garden when the whole place was packed with orphans. There were nearly fourteen thousand of these kids there as the guests of the circus

269

and the Garden managements, and the portion of the performance that we recorded was the display of sea-lion acts.

This always is a big wallop for the youngsters because the sea lions do unbelievable tricks to show off their balancing skill and they flap their "hands" together after each difficult trick to start the crowd applauding. The pay-off is when a couple of the musical sea lions put their whiskered snouts to a row of silver horns and toot "My Country 'Tis of Thee." One of the sleek, waddling "artists" plays the tune methodically and then another, with a clown-collar ruffle around his neck, steals the show by racing through the tune in jazz-time. The kids went wild. I heard the play-back before the recording was worked into the overseas broadcast and it was as exciting and thrilling as ever to listen to.

My only regret, as a sad-sack circus comic whose work is on a more sophisticated level than the antics of the more colorful, fast-moving, noisy, knock-about, whiteface clowns, is that it doesn't appeal to kids quite as much as it does to the grownups. But I've noticed that even in the laughter of the oldsters there is a strangely youthful quality.

I couldn't say that life with the circus is the softest deal in the world, but it has rewarded this country boy and I would far rather live out my life in the "alley" than in a marble palace. That's quite a concession from a "bum."

There are a few things I still look forward to: the chance to keep working at what I like best, and then, when it's all over, to see my mother drying her hands on her apron as she did when she looked at the wood pile— and to hear her say once more, "Well, you have been a fine boy and you have done a good job."

But now back to work for "Willie" and me. It's less than one minute to fanfare. The crowd is settling in the big top, Merle Evans and his men are on the bandstand and the equestrian director has his silver whistle in his hand. There's a five-second period when the whole show seems to hold its breath. Now! The shrill blast of the whistle, the cornets and the cymbals and we're rolling. Come on, "Willie"; here we go again. And do you really have to look so sad about it?

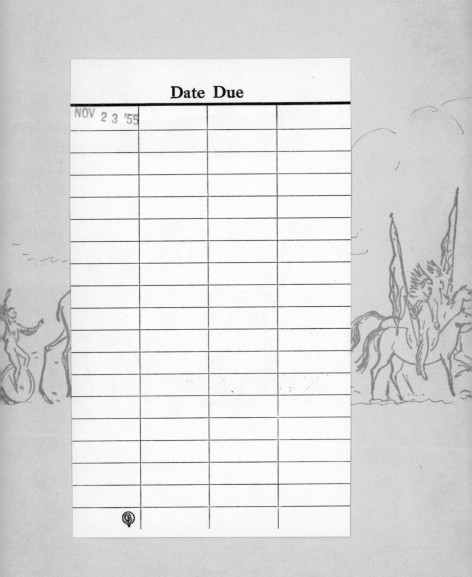

Date Due